We will never stop struggling here in the Bronx, even though they've destroyed it around us. We would pitch tents if we have to rather than move from here. We would fight back, there is nothing we would not do. They will never take us away from here. I feel very much a part of this and I'm never going to leave. And, after me, my children will be here to carry on... I have very strong children... and very strong grandchildren.

Evelina Lopez Antonetty

1922–1984
Educator, Human Rights Activist,
Advocate for Puerto Rican Independence,
Founder of United Bronx Parents
The Bronx, New York, 1980

BORN IN THE BRONX

A Visual Record of the Early Days of Hip Hop

Edited by Johan Kugelberg

Photographs by Joe Conzo
Foreword by Afrika Bambaataa
Original Flyer Art by Buddy Esquire
Featuring a Timeline by Jeff Chang

Johan thanks Joe Conzo, Grandmaster Caz, Curtis "Mexi-Ray" Sherrod, Jeff Chang, Afrika Bambaataa, Tawfiyq and Zulu Nation, Buddy Esquire, Mike Davis, Marty and the Academy Records staff, Jesper Eklow, William Gibson, Jack Womack, Blake Lethem, Andrew Upton, the Brakemen Greens Jungle crew, Gregg/Used Wax Records, Lucas McFadden, Josh Davis, Geoff Weiss, Michael Laird, Katherine Reagan, Ed Maggs, Carl Williams, Jeff Boardman and Freewheelin' Media, Jonathan Lethem, Sean Bidder, Yutaman, Kohji, Jun-Jun, One Hand Clapping, Yosushi, Stuart Baker, The Nuffer, Jonny Sklute@Goodrecordsnyc.com, Rob Corrigan @ Sound Library, Taylor Brigode, The Big Nuffer, Sean Bidder, Pogi and the Liquor, Woman and Tears crew, Sara Rosen/Powerhouse Books, Berend Dubbe, David Tibet, Caroline King And Home House, Elly, Christie, Fabel and Tools of War, Jeremy/Deadly Dragon, Bob Stanley, Charlie Ahearn, Tony Tone, Disco Wiz, Freddy Fresh, Henry Chalfant, Jamel Shabazz, Steve Stein, Justin Levy, Koe Rodriguez, Luke Caffey, Philip Mlynar, Charles, Leah, and Jacob

Johan Kugelberg

Thank you! First and foremost I thank my higher power, God, for blessing my life with family, friends, and guidance through this journey called LIFE!

Thank you Evelina Antonetty, my grandmother and "The Hell Lady of the Bronx," for instilling in me the wisdom and passion to stand up for what I believe in. Thank you Lorraine Montenegro, my mother, for giving me life and for reinforcing what Titi stood up for. Thank you Joe Conzo Sr., my father, for also giving me life and for being a role model and friend. Thank you Samantha Conzo, my wife, for believing in me and supporting me in all my dreams. To my children, Lil' Joey and Sarayna: continue the struggle to achieve your dreams, you have strong genes, I love you both! To my brothers and sisters, Eric, Jared, Stacy, and Lupe, thank you for all the love and support through the good and the bad, remembering that we are FAMILY!

To The Cold Crush Brothers, DJ Tony Tone, DJ Charlie Chase, Grandmaster Caz, Easy AD and The Almighty KG: thank you for allowing me to be a part of the Cold Crush Family. Because of your innovations and passion for the culture I'm able to share with the world true hip hop. Thank you Afrika Bambaata, The Universal Federation for the Preservation of Hip Hop, The Universal Zulu Nation, for embracing me and my passion for documenting our culture and educating our peoples.

My mentors Jamel Shabaaz, Ernie Paniccioli, Henry Chalfant, Marty Cooper, Charlie Ahearn, Joe Rodriguez, Frank Espada, Janette Beckman, Lisa Kahane, Ben Watts—thank you for embracing me and sharing your vision with me.

My 1 LOVE Family, Koe Rodriguez, Reese, Latee French, and Christy,, thank you for believing in me and for all the support!

Thank you to Sara Rosen, Bill Adler, Jeff Chang, Baldev Duggal and Rosa, David Gonzales, Elba Cabrera, Tony and Paul Mondesire, Anita and Raul Antonetty, Titi Emma, Money Ray (RIP), Tapemaster, Puerto Rico, Fabel and Christie from Tools of War, King Tone UZN, Luckystrike, Dr. Shaka Zulu, Yoda, Dragon, Joy Yoon, Kohji and Jun-Jun from BBPBX, Pogi and Yutaman, Sedgwick and Cedar, The Originator, Jeff and Freewheelin' Media, Crazy Legs and The Rocksteady Crew, Retna, Jacob and the Rizzoli Family, Jayquan, Joelee, MM, Buddy Esquire, Sal Abbatiello, Seen, PJ, Meresone, Zimad, Break, Mare139, Tracey168, James Tops, Lord Scotch, Sharp, Tats Cru, Hip Hop Connection, Superfly Magazine, waxpoetics, DJ Kool Herc, Lovebug Starski, DJ Red Alert, Mean Gene, B-boyNYC, DJ Disco Wiz, Grandwizzard Theodore, DJ Jazzy Jay, DJ Rockin' Rob, DJ Danny Dan, DJ Outlaw, DJ Yutaka, DJ Johnny Juice, DJ Lord, DJ AJ Scratch, Chuck D, Johnny Ocho, T/Ski Valley and DJ Prince, The Ghetto Brothers, The Young Lords, Whipper Whip, Mike C, The Devastating Tito, Pebble Poo, Busy Bee, LA Sunshine and Kool Moe Dee, Melle Mel and Rahiem, Rakim, Soulin, Kool G Rap, Levi, Reggie Reg, Fat Joe, Bobby Sanabria and Elena Martinez, Elinor Tatum, Micheal Kane, Ivan "Doc" Rodriguez, Julie Graham, Dr. Mark Naison, and the men and women of the greatest EMS provider in the world, the Uniformed EMTs and Paramedics of FDNY!

Johan, I cannot thank you enough, you have been another blessing in my life!

Joe Conzo

First Published in the United States of America in 2007 by
Rizzoli International Publications, Inc.
300 Park Avenue South
New York, NY 10010
www.rizzoliusa.com

Design by Mike Essl, Seth Labenz, Roy Rub

Printed in China

ISBN-13: 978-0-7893-1540-3
Library of Congress Catalog Control Number: 2007924996

CONTENTS

THE SHAKA ZULUS OF B

FUNK IN HEAVE

AT

JUNIOR HIGH SCHOOL I
(885 BOlton AVE. + Stor

FRIDAY OCT. 28, 1977

SOULSONIC

D.J. AFRIKA BAMBAA

AND THE

LISA
VANNESSA MIGHTY ZULU N

ISLAM - ED LAROCK - JILL - AUDREY -
LIL JAMES BOND. LIL BAMBAATAA - Co
CURTIS - BRUNNIE - CHARLIE ROCK - DWI
WADE - NISEY - KEELY - TERRISSA - SABRINA -
TAMISHA - ZENA - POWWOW - KHAYAN - SMITH
TWIN 1 + 2 - JAHJAH - KUSA - COWBOY - RON
MELINDA - TERRY - DEE JEE - DEE DEE - CHOY
JAJA - HOP - LEFTY - TUITT.

ONXDALE PROJECTS PRESENTS

Y IN '77

Rebecca

23

S. 131

AVE.) NEAR KORVETTS SHOPPING CENTER

— 7:00 P.M. — UNTIL???

PACE SOUNDS BY: MR. Biggs

4A & ZAMBO QUEEN KENYA

ATION DONATION: $1.50 WITH FHER

2.00 DOOR

WANA - AMIN - AMAD - SHAKA - MONK - lil

-Y - CLEAMONT - BIRDEAN - RENNE - CHIPPER-

-t - LOUIS - J.C. - JOHNNY - DONALD - SHA KING -

-SLYN - WANITA - FRANNIE - MARIA - OLUBAYO -

- AZIZ - KASHKA - TRINA - FINSTER -

D - GARY - RAYMOND - RODNEY - MARGRET-

BEAU - JUJU - MIKE - K - MIKE - CALIPH-

Super RECORD CENTER

Specializing in
AMERICAN & WEST-
INDIAN RECORDS

WE HAVE THE BEST

*DISCO *SOUL
*REGGAE
*CALYPSO *OLDIES

3432 BOSTON ROAD
OPPOSITE THE STARDUST BALL ROOM
CHECK US OUT

RECORDS ★ TAPES ★ DISCO ★ ♫
AND-NOW

Break Jam!
m.m. SOUNDS-INC.

1444 EAST Ave. (PARKCHESTER Houses.)
(Near Loews American Theatre.) ACROSS FROM MACY'S
Bronx. N.Y., 10462 -for info:call-822-8143
Lorraine - Mac
Elaine
for Break Jams see
Lenny + Bambaataa

Now Selling On The Break Jam
Market
L.P.s
8-Track
45 R.P.M.s
Cassettes

1-Bob James.   4-Breakthrough
2-Fruit SONG   5-Run Away
3-In the Slot   6-Telephone Jam

7-Think
PLEASURE-CELEBRATE
8-Opp
9-Funky President
10-Johnny theFOX
11-Commodores-Hit
AND MANY MORE JAMS

11

featuring D.J. **Afrika Bambaataa**

THE ORIGINAL D.J. **Jazzy Jay**

THE D.J. **Red Alert**

& **Soul Sonic Force** and

Mr. Biggs, Pow Wow, Lisa*Lee, Globe

Cosmic Force M.C.s

Chubby Chub, Ice Ice, Ikey "C."

ALSO D.J. **Breakout**

D.J. **Baron**

THE **Funky 4 plus 1** MORE

Doing their Hit recording THAT'S THE JOINT

Special Guest ENJOY Recording Artist

Trecherous 3 mc's

Moe·D, Special·K, La Sunshine

Doing their Recording THE BODY ROCK AT THE PARTY

D.J. GRANDMASTER **Jaz**

Invited M.C.'s B.B. Starski, Furious 5, Le Spank
fantastic 5, Sound on Sound Production, Devastating force
Super Sonic Force, THE FORCE OF THE FIVE M.C.'s

Bronx River Center

BRET BANE

FROM BAMBAATAA DEDICATED TO POPEYE, JOHNNY DYRON
Brothers

FOREWORD

Afrika Bambaataa

The Bronx went through different changes. In the 1960s, the Bronx had city planning, and organizations made sure you had city planning. You had the Blacks and Latinos in the South Bronx, Irish and Italians in the North Bronx in the Castle Hill area—and they were jumping all the way over to the West Bronx, Broadway, Kingsbridge. In between, you had us tokens living in certain areas that would get the racism, trying to "move on up" as they say in *The Jeffersons*.

You had areas like the Southeast and South Bronx with housing development projects, which were like cities in their own right. In these places, you had certain street gangs that ruled the areas, or were said to have ruled the areas, fighting for what turf was theirs. You had youth gangs that were always mixed with blacks, Puerto Ricans, Dominicans, and so forth. You had people that were searching for their roots, when so-called black people were Negroes, coloreds, and niggers, and people who spoke Spanish were spics or niggers. Then you had your radicals, your pimps and players, and hookers, and you had people who were construction workers, doctors, lawyers, nurses, taxi cab drivers.

There was politics—those trying to change life in certain parts of the Bronx, the fighters, the warriors for the community. You had people that were against the police—the radicals and revolutionaries that were part of the Black Panther Party, part of the Young Lords Party, some were even part of the crazy radical group that was blowing things up, The Weathermen. You had certain radical street gangs, some were more political, others were just to sell drugs, and others just to cause destruction. Along with that, you had a street gang within the police department called The Purple Mothers that was out to destroy the street gangs. It was made up of ex-veterans, out to assassinate them. They would take one group and stick you in an area with a group that hated you, or drop you off in a white area, and you had to make your way home—almost like the way it was in the movie *The Warriors*.

That was a time when people were fighting for their civil rights and their human rights. We had great leaders that were waking us up. From Malcolm X, Minister Farrakhan, The Most Honorable Elijah Muhammad, Huey P. Newton, Bobby Seale, Angela Davis, Richie Perez, Pablo Guzma, Dr. Malachi Z. York… They showed all of the things that the community was going through, the life and times of the struggle. So when the drug epidemic hit, messing many of our people up, people unified against it. They were together to move the drug dealers out of the community.

All this to the movement called hip hop. Hip hop saved a lot of lives, and brought the unification of many different people together under the banner of hip hop culture. There was my group, which became The Zulu Nation, and we went out and started organizing the people. I used to speak to the different leaders, the gang leaders, and the warriors for the community, and ask them to join this thing I was making. Once you get the leaders in, you start getting the followers and the members behind you, and that's how we started getting larger in the Bronx, stretching into Manhattan and the rest of the city, then to other states and the rest of the world.

You had areas that were nice and areas that were totally messed up; some would say f—ed up. It was so bad in the South Bronx, they said it was the worst place in the United States. And there was the culture of hip hop, this music. We always had the musical aspect in the Bronx. And we had the drugs, the dope, the coke—all that was plaguing the community. In going from Negro, to colored, to black, to African American, we had certain songs that used to grab the community and make everybody happy. That was the time you would see everybody do some salsa, some calypso or do each others' ways—people still trying to find their culture.

That's when books like *Down these Mean Streets* by Piri Thomas or *Man Child in the Promised Land* by Claude Brown came out, with everybody still trying to find their roots. James Brown came out with "Say it Loud, I'm Black and Proud;" Sly and the Family Stone had "Stand." You had the new birth of salsa that started to get strong on the scene, then came salsoul with brother Joe Bataan, the Joe Cuba Sextet—they were doing rap back then with that. You could see the salsa and soul at the Apollo, all of that on one stage. Joe Bataan with Dionne Warwick, the James Brown Revue and the Motown sound—all that was happening. It was a sight to see. You had the salsa, the salsoul, a lot of the calypso, Soca, reggae or ska music from the West Indies.

People get so caught up not knowing the true mentality of their roots. Like if you say you're Puerto Rican, you're still West Indian, you're still in the Caribbean. That's why there was interest in books like *Down These Mean Streets*, where you are trying to find your roots—was he black, was he Puerto Rican, was he white? Everybody was so caught up on what race or nationality you belong to, like, "If I speak Spanish, am I Hispanic?" People were trying to find themselves—and are still trying to find themselves today. But the music always played a good role in our community. With the Blacks and Latinos, every three months you had a new dance. Whites were just finding that they could get that soul, and that they got that soul. You had the radio stations, the good ones—WWRL, WLIB, WNJR, WABC.

In the black and Latino community, you're born into music. In your mother's belly, you're already feeling the vibrations of what they're feeling. The rhythm of life comes and hits you. So when you're born and take that breath of air, calling the Creator's name, you already feel the vibrations of music. By one or two, we have already started shaking something; by five, we are in full swing. Getting older, in learning to dance, you mimic adults, and then we start to do our own thing, make our own steps and dances that then come into our community.

In the early '70s, we started to bring the house turntables. In the house, you would have a whole component set, and you would have to break it all up first. You would bring this big box—or this little box—trying to put the record on. You had the spindle that dropped six 45s at one time, or you could take the spindle off and just play it manually. You had the close and play. You had the big, retarded 8-tracks, sticking out your car. When they turned to cassettes, everybody was happy because they thought this was the new thing. These 8-tracks were always clogging up all your seats, all your stuff. Before that, you had the reel-to-reel, funny radios with two channels. You would think that you were in the '40s and '50s with that type of stuff.

Then, they started getting more progressive when they started making better radios. FM came in the '70s, because it was all about AM in the '60s. FM was a cleaner, clearer sound. AM was where you would hear more about what was going on in the community. WLIB was the first black-owned radio station. Gary Byrd on WWRL used to do the GBE, the Gary Byrd Experience. There was Cousin Brucie on WABC.

We always had rap in our community. You had Joe Cuba, Gil Scott-Heron, Last Poets. Shirley Ellis with "The Clapping Song," "The Name Game," Pigmeat Markham, who came up with "Here Comes the Judge." You also had your rock records that had a rap to them, like "Mama Told Me Not To Come/Joy To The World." Sly and the Family Stone had a rap on their second album. There was rapping that was done on the radio. You can see how far the rapping, call-and-response thing goes back, even before our time. Back to Cab Calloway and all those cats, all the way to Isaac Hayes and Barry White. You had the poet-rappers—Wanda Robinson, Maya Angelou, Last Poets.

It was basically from seeing so many great teachers that came and taught us how to unify, knowing how to speak to our people, going into different communities, saying let's make something happen. That, and giving community parties, as well as what we added in the '80s, what we called the fifth element: knowledge. You had that strong black core. That was a time when we would respect each other's momma. Certain people had that status in the community—don't mess around, you'll get your butt whipped. It was interesting to see how these things started to change into the disrespect, or how the brainwashing techniques have started to seep in this day and time, where the youth will just cuss or even try to make a move on their elders, when they are trying to teach them something.

It's thirty-three years for the Universal Zulu Nation, thirty-two years for what we're calling hip hop culture, but it goes even further than that to years when we might of said the "go-off," or the "be-bop," when it didn't have no name. Add the Zulu Nation's years to the Black Spades' five or six, and it's really been organized for quite a while now. Hip hop keeps it all together, but you know it's the fifth element that gets people from different nationalities and places to speak about different subjects—mythologies, AIDS, diseases, politics, the universe, subterranean worlds.

That's the interesting part, changing different views, the ideologies, respecting all of the different religions. It's something where, whether it's right or wrong, we can sit and talk to each other—and not kill each other. You're dealing with a machine that is controlling the minds of the masses and keeping the people in poverty, teaching them to be greedy, stealing from each other's lands. That is the cause for so much of the chaos on our planet today. People of color get sick and tired and start to rise, and the people in power see this rising and try to hold on to power, doing all types of evilness in the name of their Creator to keep their power.

Everybody talks about the war in Iraq. These people love Allah the Supreme Force, where others claim to love Jesus, but do everything except what's in the Bible book. Everybody says that this is my holy book, but they don't really follow it, so who are you following?

People got to go back and research who they are, their roots, and what happened. The biggest thing is the fear factor. They have made it now so you're fearful to open your mouth, or to protest. When they first started the war, everybody thought if you were against the war, you would lose your job, they would lock you up. Everybody was nervous at first. But then you see the people get tired, the people hitting the streets again, all races and nationalities hitting it. People are still wondering how Bush stole the election. What is really going on in your government, and what's really behind your government, and who is controlling your mind, using mind control tactics? We've got to reevaluate what is really going on.

In Africa, there is no way that anybody should go hungry, starving there, when the Creator blessed Africa with everything in it, every animal and being in it, the farmland, the trees. Who is paying all that money to make sure that Africa stays starving or messed up when the whole world took their civilization from Africa? And really, for everyone on the planet, their mother really is African, if they go back and check the roots of it all.

The people in power are tricking the people; that they've got you under their rule, that you are my Hispanic, you are my black. If you try to go find it, where is black land, white land, yellow land, brown land, red land—you can't find it. It's really about your status and your nationality and where you come from. Humans are the only ones that have this bugged out thing—that they are colors. Everybody has a place set for us, where we won't be ourselves. They have wiped out history, yourstory, ourstory.

When our Spanish brother says, "Look at that Mureno, or the Moor/Muur," you don't know that you are Mureno, too. It's going to take a big cleaning of our minds, our mentality, to go back to what it was like when people were trying to wake up, because they have done a great brainwash job on all of us, to make us hate ourselves or be fearful of ourselves. Or we have to move into their community to say that we finally made it, that we're "moving on up," like *The Jeffersons*.

Afrika Bambaataa
2007

CELEBRITY
CLUB
35 EAST 125 ST. MAN
BETWEEN PARK + MADISON
EASTER
SUNDAY
Live and in person
Grand Master
FLASH
FURIOUS 5
DISCO   EZ
BEE   MIKE
PLUS
KOOL DJ AJ
CHIEF ROCKER
BUSY BEE
E-MAN
GRAND WIZARD THEODORE
FANTASTIC 5 MCS
LADIES $5.   9 UNTIL
MEN $6.   APRIL 6
NO. FIVE TRAIN

50.00
FOR
BEST
DRESS

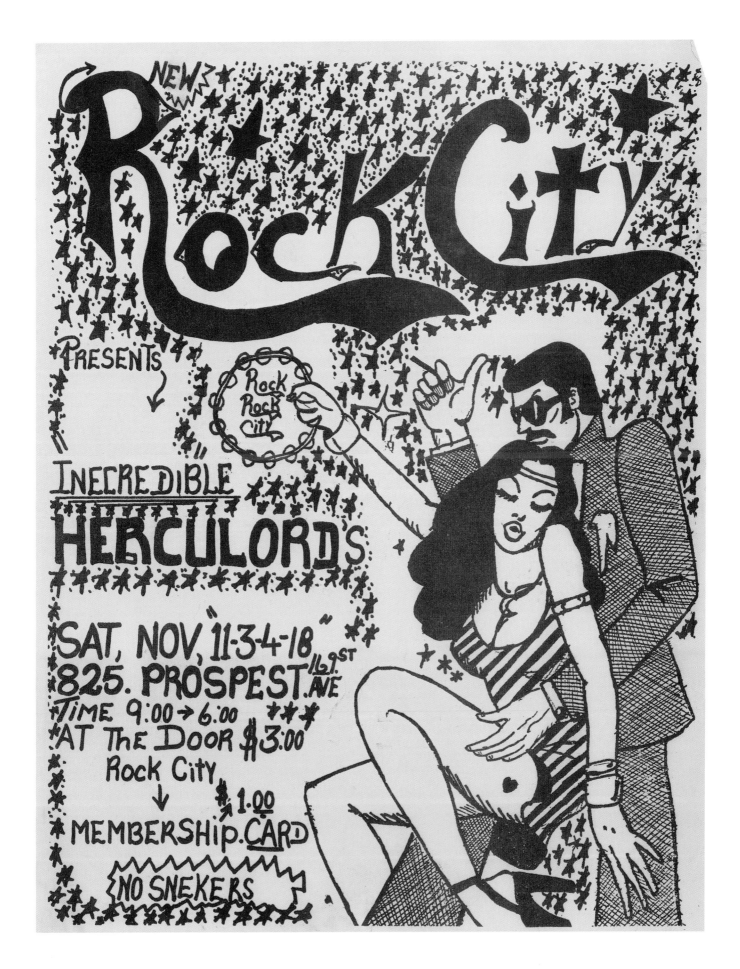

Grandmaster FLASH Furious.5

Mele Mel Mr Ness Cowboy Kidd Creole Rahiem
DISCOBEE EZMIKE

"2 Superstar Crews battle it out for NY's Number One!"

Brothers Disco Dj BREAK
Funky 4 + 1 More ®

No.1 Female Mc **Sha Rock K K Rockwell Jazzy J**
Lil Rodney C Keith Keith

T Connection
3510 Wht. Plns. Rd.
May 2, 1980 10 Until

$6 Guys $5C

F.

T.M.F. PRODUCTIONS
presents

THE GRAND
MASTER
CASANOVA FLY
and
THE DISCO WIZ
&
D.J. MIGHTY MIKE
featuring
A 1 FEMALE D.J. PAM-BAA-TAA
PLACE TO BE

4529 3RD AVE. BET.
183 & 182
(JUNE 15.....THUR. 7:pm TO 2:AM)
adm $1.00

(JUNE 17......FRI. 10:pm UNTIL)
adm $2.00

INTRODUCTION

The idea of this book is to present a snapshot of the early days of hip hop. It is not comprehensive, nor has it set out to be. Rather, what I hope to accomplish is an impressionistic narrative, a state of mind, a daydream of what it might have been likc, what it could have felt like, and a sense of the extraordinary vibrancy and urgency of these times. I am interested in the sense of wonder that positively shines out of these images. I want to bring to the reader a feeling of immersion in this art and this culture that is similar to my own ten-year journey. I wasn't there, and as an outsider I am not trying to present a watertight historical account of this period in hip hop's history. That is a job for someone who was there, and I am confident that the next decade will see a slew of fascinating books that do so—some, I hope, by the pioneers themselves.

I am in awe of this grass-roots culture, the Bronx of the 1970s. I have no deep roots in hip hop—back then, I was into punk rock and skateboarding, which colors the perspective I bring to this book. The punk movement, which is an obvious parallel to early hip hop, is far less impressive to my mind: where the middle-class roots of punk (notwithstanding the working-class posturing of many of its originators) provided an apparatus of self-importance and self-documentation that had someone hang on to a copy of the gig flyer, or make a list of the people present, or interview the band for their fanzines, or be the self-appointed scene photographer, early rap was truly and simply the essence of a local, performance-based culture. Punk, ultimately, was driven by products; early hip hop was driven by Saturday night.

The skateboarding subculture, which invokes the same problematic dynamic of rebel culture and corporate branding that in 2007 infuses almost every aspect of hip hop, has a similar structure of origin. Something is brought from an island far away (Hawaii, or Jamaica) to an environment where the extremes of material wealth rub shoulders (Malibu vs. Santa Monica, or the Bronx vs. Manhattan), and the youth create something out of nothing because that is their only option (nailing old roller skates onto planks of wood, or rhyming over the breaks on their parents' James Brown records).

But unlike skateboarding or punk, hip hop was not self-documenting. The tyranny of the new in the ghetto creates a climate where the acts of looking, writing, or thinking of past times can be considered counterproductive. Progress, wealth, innovation—the future is where it's at, and glancing in the rear-view mirror can get you stuck. It seems that this idea applies mostly to recent history, and that a lifetime must pass before critical merit or historical significance is attributed to scholarship in the fields of entertainment or pop culture. A parallel can be traced in the scattershot scholarship of jazz and blues in the years prior to the resurgence of interest in the late 1950s: the vanguard of the field was driven by fans, by record collectors, by enthusiasm, and was usually far removed from the community itself. Luckily, this is no longer the case in the field of studying hip hop.

The chief challenge that faces those of us who attempt to document the early days of hip hop is that artifacts are practically nonexistent. When Mike Davis of Academy Records introduced me to Curtis Sherrod—better known to you all as Mexi-Ray of the Nice & Nasty Three—I was given access to a massive collection of hip hop flyers that became a large portion of the artwork in this book. These flyers tell us the when and where. When I met Buddy Esquire, and gained access to his archive, we were able to observe the truly complex design techniques utilized by this master of the hip hop show flyer, where rulers, markers, and rub-on letters were used to create astounding graphic effects in the days before desktop design. And when Grandmaster Caz, arguably one of the greatest MCs of all time, introduced me to master photographer Joe Conzo and his previously unseen archive of thousands of images shot in hip hop's very infancy, the epiphany of seeing what these people and events looked like inspired a newfound sense of connection to these vibrant early days. We could add the who to the when and where.

"It doesn't really matter who rapped first as long as the rap satisfies your thirst."
—Mike T., "Do It Any Way You Wanna" (Golden Pyramid)

The narratives in this book are not intended to give specifics of what happened when, or who was first, what's on second or I don't knows on third… Although there is certainly a substantial amount of what Afrika Bambaataa calls "factology" to be found within, that is not a central goal of these stories. They are meant to give us outsiders (and you insiders) a feel for the time and a sense of what it meant to the people who were there. The book is meant to be impressionistic, an experience that envelops us in an emotional response to visuals that mimics what we feel when we hear music. As I was editing images and text, and deciding on their sequence for this book, I worked to a soundtrack of the following records: Baby Huey's "Listen To Me," Lonnie Love's "Young Ladies," Nice & Nasty Three's "The Ultimate Rap," Cold Crush Brothers' "Weekend," Grandwizzard Theodore and the Fantastic Romantic Five's "Can I Get A Soul Clap (Straight Out Of The Pack)," Afrika Bambaataa's "Planet Rock (Addams Family mix)," Danny Renee and Charisma Crew's "Space Rap," and, naturally, the Incredible Bongo Band's "Apache," the unofficial anthem of the Boogie Down Bronx. I suggest you do the same.

I am proud to present Joe Conzo's amazing photographs, taken between 1977 and 1982—years in the development of hip hop of which we had very few images until now. Buddy Esquire's flyer designs are masterpieces of eyeball-pleasing efficiency. Tony Tone's Polaroids and Charlie Ahearn's photographs are rare finds that bring another intimate component to this visual narrative. All this, and the Cold Crush Brothers ephemera, and the assortment of early show flyers, combine to create a sense of this stage in the evolution of a Bronx-born art form. And in my wildest dreams I would never have thought that this book would have been honored with a foreword by Afrika Bambaataa. I am awestruck that this great man, this spiritual community leader, would grace our pages. He continues to inspire, to motivate, and to make things happen for generation after generation of musicians, artists, writers, and thinkers.

For me, the most important part of all this is that it showcases a self-starting culture. If you are a sixteen-year-old looking at this book, or if you remember the confusion of what that was like, you should know that all of us are capable of accomplishing our life goals and desires. You can be an MC, you can be a brain surgeon, you can be an astronaut, you can be a quarterback, you can be a chartered accountant or a pony salesman. Whatever you set out to do, you can do. This book is evidence: with hip hop, born in the Bronx, these guys created something out of nothing. That's amazing. That's alchemy. That's magic.

Johan Kugelberg
Amsterdam, Spring 2007

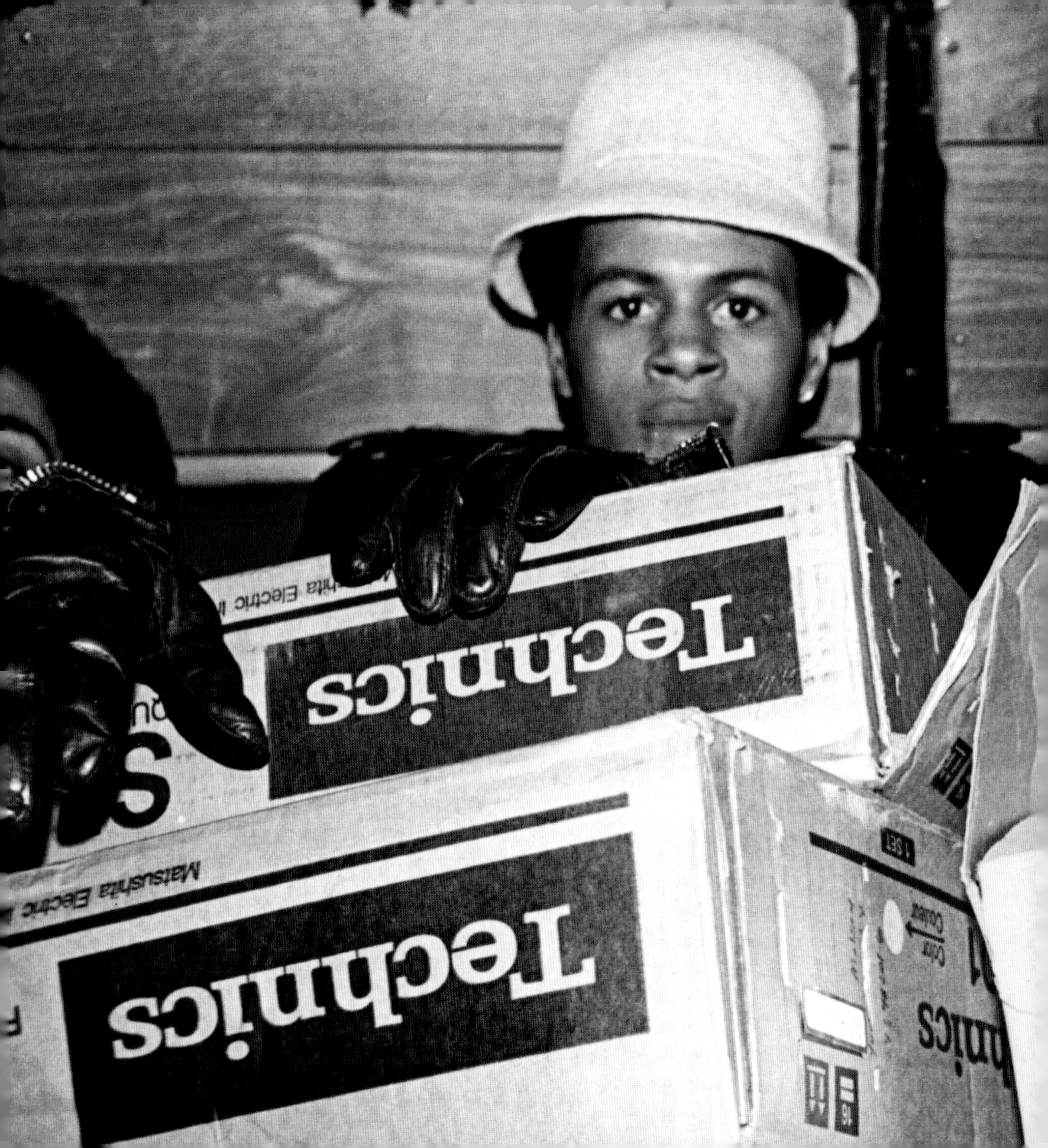
Technics
Matsushita Electric
Technics

THE BRONX

The Black Door, one of the Bronx's earliest hip hop venues.

The beauty of the Bronx of the 1940s and 1950s can be difficult to comprehend if your view of the area is defined by images of the 1970s of block after block of rubble and burned-out buildings. But back in the years following the Second World War, an influx of African-American and Latin immigrants settling in the Bronx met with wide streets and formidable houses. It took only a few years for these comfortable working-class neighborhoods to transform into raging, desperate slums.

The beginning of the end was 1959, when the city began to build an expressway straight through the Bronx that cut down everything small, nice, and neighborhood-like in its path toward a "progress" that sacrificed the local for a diffuse greater good. The middle-class population of the Bronx left pretty much overnight, an exodus which led to the impoverished portion of the population spreading further and further north from their enclave in the South Bronx. Businesses and factories started to relocate. By 1969, Robert Moses' housing behemoth Co-Op City was completed. This gigantic complex, situated in the northernmost part of the Bronx, and serviced by one of Moses' freeways, meant that the small remainder of a Bronx middle class was now completely gone.

All the horrors of urban blight reached their acme in the Bronx of 1970. Crime was rampant: street gangs had mushroomed all over the borough and made it dangerous to move from block to block on foot, even in the daytime. Between 1970 and 1975, gangs ruled the Bronx. The Black Spades (including a future Afrika Bambaataa), the Savage Skulls, the Royal Charmers, the Savage Nomads, and others too numerous to mention waged continual turf wars (contemporary sources estimated the number of gangs to be between 250 and 300, with a total of more than 20,000 members). With the desperation of those who have nothing, they harmed and sometimes killed their own, instead of uniting against the forces that oppressed them.

Some gangs, like the Ghetto Brothers, embarked upon a variety of community outreach programs, ranging from free breakfasts for children to schemes designed to chase out drug dealers from neighborhoods. As usual, however, when history is told things aren't what they seem, and the "good" do bad things and the "bad" do things for the greater good of the community.

J.K.

Map of hip hip New York c. 1979, by Charlie Ahearn

NOV 6, 84

It HigH School

A Crowd of 4,000 people

one the move
SH four Rockin the House

TIMELINE

Jeff Chang

Bronxite Willie Colon and Hector Lavoe record *El Malo*, a record that heralds the emergence of the streetwise Nuyorican sound of salsa.

In New Orleans, the Meters record their hugely influential first two albums, *The Meters* and *Look-Ka Py-Py*.

Inspired by the Black Panthers, the Young Lords Party is founded in Spanish Harlem to call attention to the plight of Puerto Ricans.

High-ranking New York City official Roger Starr articulates the influential idea of "planned shrinkage," a proposal to remove services from "sick neighborhoods" such as the Bronx, primarily poor and non-white communities.

The top 21 Black Panthers in New York City are arrested, including Afeni Shakur.

Clyde Stubblefield gets some on James Brown's *Funky Drummer*, which became one of the most sampled records of all time.

The completion of the Cross-Bronx Expressway ushers in a rapid decline in the Bronx. Housing stock, devalued by the building of the highway, further declines as landlords sometimes turn to arson to collect insurance money. Half of the white population flees the borough in the next decade.

Clive Campbell immigrates to the Bronx from Kingston, Jamaica.

1966

1968

1963

1967

1969

In a memo, FBI chief J. Edgar Hoover directs COINTELPRO (counterintelligence program) to destroy the Nation of Islam and the Black Panther Party.

The sound of Bugalu—featuring artists like Joe Bataan, Joe Cuba, Pete "Conde" Rodriguez, who blend African-American and Latino rhythms and styles—replaces doo-wop as the sound of the Bronx.

United Bronx Parents, a community organization dedicated to improving the conditions of people living in the South Bronx, is incorporated by Dr. Evelina Lopez Antonetty, and becomes the moral center of the neighborhood through its ongoing struggles.

Heroin floods the streets of the south and southeast Bronx.

After a tumultuous election season, Richard Nixon is elected in a backlash against the student movement and the Great Society programs.

Robert Moses caps his transformation of the Bronx and New York City with the opening of Co-Op City, towering apartment buildings in the far southeast Bronx.

1970

- Many families begin moving from the arson-devastated South Bronx to the West Bronx.

- With the Panthers behind bars and the Young Lords retreating to Puerto Rico, gangs increase their influence on the streets of the Bronx.

- DJ Kool Herc invents the "merry-go-round," a form of spinning breakbeats back-to-back, and forms the Herculords with his pal, the first hip-hop era rapper, Coke La Rock.

- The OPEC oil crisis results in long gas line chaos and economic downturns across the U.S.

- A front-page article in the *New York Times* discusses tagger TAKI 183, and suddenly hundreds of youths want to be taggers too.

- Richard Goldstein's "This Thing Has Completely Gotten Out of Hand" in *New York Magazine* offers the first serious coverage—and defense—of the subway graffiti movement.

- New York City's two largest gangs—the largely African-American Black Spades and the largely Nuyorican Savage Skulls—go to war.

- Cindy Campbell throws a back-to-school party at Sedgwick & Cedar; her brother DJ Kool Herc spins records.

- After the killing of a gang peacemaker from the Ghetto Brothers, representatives of 42 gangs come together to sign an unprecedented peace treaty. While gang violence continues to be a serious problem into the mid-70s, the circumstances of the Bronx peace treaty make the emergence of hip-hop culture possible.

- Afrika Bambaataa's Zulu Nation forms and begins actively recruiting outcast black and Latino youths in the south and southeast Bronx under a banner of "Peace, Love, Unity, and Having Fun."

1972

1974

1971

1973

- Daniel Moynihan writes in a memo to President Richard Nixon, "The time may have come when the issue of race could benefit from a period of 'benign neglect'."

- James Brown brings in the Collins brothers to record new versions of "Sex Machine" and "Give It Up Or Turn It Loose" that define the sound of the classic funk breakbeat, a new fusion of clave- and blues-based rhythms.

- Youth gangs proliferate in south and southeast Bronx neighborhoods already devastated by deindustrialization, disinvestment, white flight, and widespread arson.

- The Young Lords and members of the Savage Skulls, Savage Nomads, and Ghetto Brothers join to take over Lincoln Hospital for a day to bring attention to the terrible quality of health care provided to Bronx residents.

- DJ Kool Herc takes his parties indoors into West and East Bronx clubs like The Twilight Zone and The Hevalo.

- Norman Mailer's ode to tagging, *The Faith of Graffiti*, is published.

- The first-ever graffiti exhibition is organized by Hugo Martinez at City College of New York.

- Joe Conzo takes his first photograph.

- The Ghetto Brothers release their album, *Power Fuerza*.

- Michael Viner's Incredible Bongo Band records a wild version of "Apache" featuring Bahamian bongo player King Errisson. It bombs everywhere but the Bronx, where it is later picked up by a young DJ named Kool Herc.

- The writer's corner at 149th Street begins, started by writers like PHASE 2, BLADE, PISTOL, and others. Stylistic innovation explodes on the subway trains over the next year.

- SUPER KOOL 223 does the first masterpiece and top-to-bottom car.

Afrika Bambaataa's cousin Soulski is killed by police, firming his resolve to advance peace efforts through Zulu Nation.

Grandmaster Flash, using his Clock Theory and Quickmix technique, perfects the art of mixing and blending breakbeats.

Grandwizzard Theodore discovers the scratch.

Charlie Chase begins DJ-ing in the Bronx, bringing together African-American funk crowds and Puerto Rican disco crowds at his parties.

The warm months after the riots bring the peak of the Bronx block party era.

The Rock Steady Crew is founded in the Bronx by Jo Jo and Jimmy D.

Music journalist Robert Ford makes the first mention of the rap phenomenon in club reports in his R&B column for *Billboard* magazine.

Women's crews and stars abound: the Zulu Queens B-Girl Crew, the Mercedes Ladies, as well as DJ Wanda Dee, and MCs Lisa Lee, Sha-Rock, Little Lee, Sweet and Sour, Debbie D, and Pebblee Poo.

According to Johan Kugelberg, the first breakbeat record is made: a 45 single credited to Yvette and the Kids that is simply a loop of "Funky Drummer."

Jimmy Carter visits Charlotte Street.

"Rappers Delight" explodes as an international hit.

Freeway Rick buys his first bag of cocaine.

The Fatback Band's *King Tim III (Personality Jock)* becomes the first rap record to chart in Billboard.

Joe Bataan's "Rap-O Clap-O" becomes the first rap hit in Europe. It fails to catch on in the U.S.

Mr. Magic hosts the first rap radio show *Mr. Magic's Disco Showcase* on WHBI 105.9 in New York City.

Academic Nathan Glazer's article "On Subway Graffiti in New York" in *Public Interest Journal* becomes the foundation for neoconservative "broken windows" theory and what becomes urban "quality of life" policies and "zero tolerance" policing during the '90s in American cities.

Cold Crush lineup is finally set: Charlie Chase, Tony Tone, Grandmaster Caz, JDL, Almighty KG.

Grandmaster Flash and the Furious 4 crush the Brothers Disco and The Funky 4 at the PAL. The Funky 4 temporarily dissolve and Raheim becomes a member of the newly renamed Furious 5.

Backed by Ford, Moore, and Russell Simmons, Kurtis Blow secures first rap major label deal for "Christmas Rappin."

After the President refuses to help New York City resolve its massive municipal bankruptcy crisis, the *New York Daily News* headline reads, "Ford to City: Drop Dead!"

The great blackout of New York initiates riots throughout the city.

The Yankees win the World Series behind a historic performance by Reggie Jackson in the Bronx.

1976

1978

1980

1975

1977

1979

Bambaataa mixing it up with Fela, Kraftwerk.

The original cast soundtrack of the Broadway play *Runaways* features what may be the first modern rap on record.

DJ Hollywood, Pete DJ Jones, Reggie Wells, June Bug, Eddie Cheeba, and Grandmaster Flowers mark the heyday of the disco rap DJs, particularly in Uptown clubs like Club 371 and Harlem World, and venues like the Audubon Ballroom, and Brooklyn Soundsystems.

Charlie Chase, Cisco, RC, T-Bone, Grandmaster Caz, Whipper Whip, Tony Tone, Easy AD, and Dota Rock form the Cold Crush Brothers.

Whipper Whip and Dota Rock leave the Cold Crush to join Kevie Kev (Waterbed Kev), and L Brothers (Mean Gene and Grandwizzard Theodore) to form the Fantastic Romantic 5.

Inspired by Phase 2, Buddy Esquire designs his first flyer. Other important flyer artists include Eddie Ed, Beck, and Aton E.

Charlie Ahearn works on super 8 martial arts movie *The Deadly Art Of Survival* with Nathan Ingram with murals by Lee Quiñones, which leads to the making of *Wild Style*.

Afrika Bambaataa's first official party as DJ at the Bronx River Community Center.

Grandmaster Flash packs the Audobon with DJ AJ opening.

The film *Assault on Precinct 13* ushers in racial urban horror genre. The genre reaches its apotheosis in *The Warriors*.

Grandmaster Flash and the Three MCs—Cowboy, Kid Creole, Melle Mel—take up residency at the Black Door club.

Lenny Roberts introduced to the breakbeats by his son who is a member of Zulu Nation, goes on to sell Cutout Break records, then produces the Octopus Breaks then Ultimate Breaks and Beats series with the help of Afrika Bambaataa.

B-boying undergoes changes, from styles practiced by African-American dancers like the Twins to styles rooted in Afro-Latin dance traditions practiced by Puerto Ricans like Spy.

The Cold Crush Brothers play Joe Conzo's graduation prom at South Bronx High School.

Henry Chalfant holds an exhibition of his subway art photographs at the OK Harris Gallery, giving the movement important exposure in liberal art circles.

Countercultural collective Colab mounts the *Times Square Show* in an abandoned brothel, one of the first major shows for Jean-Michel Basquiat, Keith Haring, Fab 5 Freddy and Lee Quiñones.

At the *Times Square Show*, Charlie Ahearn, Fab 5 Freddy, and Lee Quiñones meet and agree to work on the first hip hop movie, *Wild Style*.

The People's Convention opens on Charlotte Street. Its organizers include future politician Jose Rivera.

Ronald Reagan visits Charlotte Street, using the same words Jimmy Carter had uttered 3 years before.

Freeway Rick cuts cocaine with baking soda to make "ready rock," later named "crack" by the media.

Kurtis Blow, the first rapper signed to a major label, sees his single, "The Breaks," become the first rap to be officially certified gold.

In an October 1980 *Soul Train* appearance, Kurtis Blow becomes the first rapper on U.S. TV. The Funky 4 + 1 follow soon after with an appearance on *Saturday Night Live*.

Bronx Puerto Ricans and African-Americans launch protests against the Paul Newman movie, *Fort Apache: The Bronx*.

Shooting begins on *Wild Style*—Busy Bee, Cold Crush Brothers, Fantastic 5, Grand Master Flash, and the Rock Steady Crew participate.

DJ Whiz Kid becomes the first winner of the New Music Seminar DJ Battle.

Afrika Bambaataa begins using the term "hip hop," popularized in parties by Lovebug Starski, to refer to the street youth cultures emerging from the Bronx and other New York communities of color.

Kool Lady Blue starts hosting "Wheels of Steel" night at Negril nightclub, downtown Manhattan.

ABC's *20/20* airs "Rappin' To The Beat." The piece is an in-depth look into hip-hop culture, featuring a young Rock Steady Crew.

One of the most famous old-school battles: the Cold Crush Brothers take on the Fantastic 5 at Harlem World.

ABC's *20/20* news program covers the Lincoln Center battle between Rock Steady Crew and the Dynamic Rockers, the first instance of national network coverage of hip-hop.

Feature stories on hip hop's explosion at The Roxy appear in *Rolling Stone*, *Life*, and *People* magazines.

After creating a huge buzz in New York City, Charlie Ahearn's *Wild Style* goes into national release.

Wild Style world premiere in Tokyo, Japan, with Cold Crush Brothers, Busy Bee, Double Trouble, Rock Steady Crew, Fab 5 Freddy, Charlie Ahearn, Futura, Dondi, among others.

Run DMC's first single, "It's Like That"/"Sucker MCs," heralds a new sound in rap music, an end to the old school.

In Los Angeles, Freeway Rick Ross standardizes the sale and distribution of crack cocaine to the masses.

With appearances by members of the Rock Steady Crew, *Flashdance* becomes the first Hollywood movie to feature b-boying.

A new hardcore sound hits the streets in the form of Philadelphia rapper Schoolly D's "P.S.K." and Los Angeles rapper Toddy Tee's "Batteram."

Crack cocaine use reaches epidemic proportions in Los Angeles, Miami, and New York City.

Tagger Michael Stewart is killed by MTA police in the New York subway.

The widely-panned Sidney Janis Gallery exhibition *Post-Graffiti* marks the end of the art world's short-lived flirtation with graffiti writers.

Jesse Jackson announces his first presidential bid.

Brian DePalma's *Scarface* is released.

LL Cool J's *Radio* becomes the first album released by a label called Def Jam through a major label distribution deal with Columbia Records.

1982

1984

1986

1981

1983

1985

Run DMC's self-titled debut album becomes the first rap album to be officially certified gold.

Bernhard Goetz shoots 4 black male teens on a New York subway.

The New York City Rap Tour—featuring Afrika Bambaataa, the Rock Steady Crew, Futura, Dondi, Grandmixer D.St., Rammellzee, and Fab 5 Freddy and organized by Roxy promoter Kool Lady Blue— goes to England and France.

The *Fresh Fest* tour featuring Run DMC, Kurtis Blow, the Fat Boys, Newcleus, Whodini, Dynamic Breakers, and the Magnificent Force becomes the first major national rap tour, hitting 27 cities and grossing $3.5 million.

Grandmaster Flash and the Furious 5's record "The Message," actually written and performed by Sugarhill songwriter Duke Bootee and Melle Mel, becomes a huge hit.

The Roxy, a massive roller rink on the Westside, opens for *Wheels of Steel* night.

The pilot of Michael Holman's *Graffiti Rock*, a hip-hop take on *Soul Train* and *American Bandstand*, debuts. It doesn't get picked up.

Run DMC's *Raising Hell* becomes the first rap album to be officially certified platinum.

During their triumphant *Raising Hell* tour, Run DMC encounter a full-blown gang melee in progress at the Long Beach auditorium.

Afrika Bambaataa and the Soulsonic Force release *Planet Rock* on Tom Silverman's Tommy Boy Records. It goes on to sell 650,000 copies.

Tony Silver and Henry Chalfant's documentary *Style Wars* airs on PBS across the country, prompting sporadic protests from some angry viewers.

In Los Angeles, ground-breaking 24 hour rap radio station KDAY goes on the air.

Mandatory minimum sentencing is established for crack cocaine users through the Federal Anti-Drug Abuse Act of 1986. The result is a racially disparate explosion in the prison population in the U.S.

The first Reagan recession brings widespread joblessness to inner cities across the U.S.

Wild Style screened for the first time in 16mm.

The publication of first important books on hip-hop include Steven Hager's *Hip Hop* and David Toop's *Rap Attack*, followed closely by *Fresh* co-written by Nelson George, Sally Banes, Susan Flinker, and Patty Romanowski.

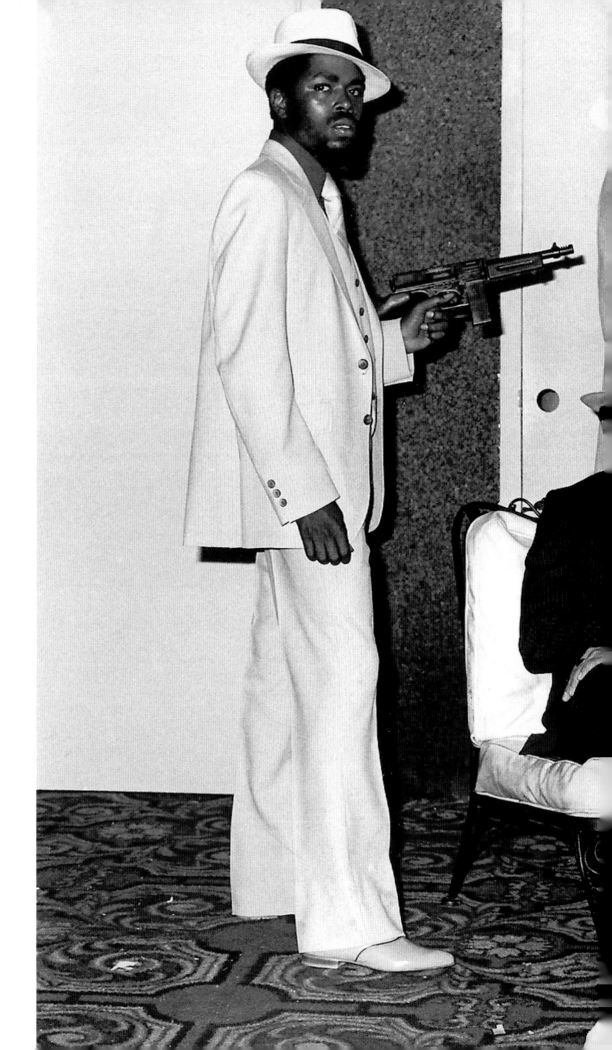

Pen & Scroll MILITARY FRATERNITY
presents

A
Pre-Easter Disco

FEATURING THE DYNAMIC SOUNDS of

D.J.
HOLLYWOOD!

ON TUESDAY EVENING: APR. 1, 1980
at
CADET HEADQUARTERS - FROM - 10:00 PM TO 4:00 AM

Positively
NO
Sneakers
Admitted!!!

WITH TICKET $7.00

We reserve
the
right to be
Selective.

WITH TICKET $7.00

To Mexi - Ray

ORLANDO PRODUCTIONS PRESENTS
ANOTHER
"COLD CRUSHER JAM"
TNT AND THE CLIENTELE BROTHERS

LARRY GEE "THE MIXORCIST"
DOLLAR BILL "THE MELLOW ROCK"
EDDIE O'JAY "KING OF RHYME"
MR. GENE "THE MIX MACHINE"
STEADY BEE "RAPOLOGIST"

VS.

T-PRODUCTIONS

VS.

SOUL CONTROL

3 SEPARATE SOUND SYSTEMS

$3 Before 10:00 P.M.

Saturday May 16, 1981
AT
The St. Gertudes Center 338 Beach 38TH St.
Far Rockaway, Queens

Directions: Take the (A) train to Beach 36 st. Edgmere, or take the (E) or (F) train to Parsons Blvd. and take the Q 113 bus to the last stop, then walk or take Green line bus to 38th st.

FLYER: LARRY GEE 81.

THE EPHEMERAL BEAUTY OF HIP HOP FLYERS

The whole nature of the firsts of hip hop is clear in general, if not in specifics. With a twenty-five year perspective on the art form, questions concerning the true originators, the creation of the form, and contributors to its evolution can be answered relatively easily. Things get blurry only when you try to trace the histories of specific firsts: first MC, first scratcher on record, first live jam, first indoor jam, and, naturally, the first hip hop record. Small record companies run by independent entrepreneurs hustling to make a buck don't keep detailed documentation on the records they release.

So how do we find out as much as we can about this seminal period in pop-cultural history? Well, those of us who weren't there have to go to the source material—and there is not much source material to be had, nor has there ever been. There are battle tapes and some rudimentary and truly marginal print-media coverage, and then there are flyers. The crude beauty of the battle tapes is awesome, and speaking for those of us who have the Cold Crush vs. Fantastic Five tape, I cannot think of any hip hop on record that comes close to that intensity. The battle tapes don't answer any whos, whats, or wheres, though—but the flyers certainly do.

Jon Savage, in his book *England's Dreaming* (the definitive tome on UK punk, sports fans), speaks eloquently and lengthily about the advent of Xerox culture—where images could be duplicated quickly en masse based on a simple monochrome design on colored paper, printed cheaply at the corner deli or at your uncle's office, for a mere penny a pop or nothing at all if you were lucky. According to Curtis Sherrod, editions of flyers could run anywhere from a couple of hundred to 10,000 or more for some of the bigger events. "So why are they so goddamn rare, then?" asks Rutger the b-boy from his crib in Krakow. The reason lies in their ephemeral nature: they were handed out in schoolyards and in lunch rooms, stacks of them were left in delis or laundromats, or handed out on subway trains. Ephemeral like last week's grocery list, ephemeral like mash notes to your eighth-grade girlfriend, ephemeral like yesterday's *New York Post.* People threw them away or traded them in at the door for a discount.

The flyers are things of extraordinary beauty. Ranging from the work of original masters of the form, Phase 2 and Buddy Esquire, to hoards of anonymous flyer artistes, this truly was the last gasp of pre-desktop publishing design. Stencils, rub-on letters, those plastic rulers with the outlines of letters, cuttings from newspapers and comic books, cartoon drawings, sometimes crude, sometimes technically brilliant, all collaged into artwork that positively shivers with electric vitality, even now, more than a quarter-century later.

J.K.

The Dead Sea Scroll of hip hop: a flyer for a 1973 Kool Herc jam.

Seven years later, the simple dates and times of primitive flyers had been replaced by designs as elaborate as this Buddy Esquire masterpiece.

B-Beats
Here

★

Grand Wiza
Theodore
Fantastic 5
MASTER Rob
'ORIGINAL
Kevie Kev
Rubie Dee
Dota Rock*
Whipper Wh
back by popular D

Saint Mark Alumni Club Presents:

Grand Masters Production

Rock-it!

Throwdown with the sound!

D.J.'S:

Scorpio

Miestro

Def Trio M.C.'s:

Bobby D

Jimmy J

Kool J.C.

D. Gray 1979

Bishop Perry Hall (#4 train – 149th change to #2 train – 135th)
(#5 train – 149th change to #2 train – 135th)

65 West 138 Street

Bet. Lenox & 5th ave

Friday, Jan. 18, 1980

9:00pm – 1:00am.

$2.00 with Flyer

$2.50 without Flyer

Prizes   Prizes

"The Weekend"   By: Grand Master Caz

We're the Cold Crush Four give-a-givin
you more and we just came to say
Ooh, Aah what a relief it is
when the weekend comes your way

So grab a chair from anywhere
and listen while we speak
Cause the fours gonna start this record
off with the first day of the week

<u>Monday</u>: The train was late and you
hardly ate and you wish
you'd stayed in bed

<u>Tuesday</u>: You ran a game on your favorite
dame and she left and messed
up your head

AD PART

<u>Wednesday</u>: You tried to be cool you stayed
out of school yeah
You fronted and showboated

<u>Thursday</u>: Now your minds in doubt
you cant figure out
Why your not gonna get

promoted

All
Friday: After your work is through
you sleep for a few
Till you hear somebody say

All Wake Up, Wake Up, now don't you know

All   The weekend when we Play
Jeday is Saturday Huh! BREAK

CA2 It's Saturday night and you're ready
to show
JDC At the place where all the fly people go

A> You've been working at school
or your occupation
KG Now its about time for some recreation

CA2 Slip on your shirt and designer jeans
JDC The ones that are tight at the hips and
the seams
A> You shoot out the door like you're runnin
a race
KG Then you finally arrive at the party place

And BREAK

I'm Easy A.D. not talkin no jive
and the party's gonna swing when
I arrive

Well, I'm the Almighty and when, I get
there
I wanna hear everybody cheer, cheer, cheer

All And we're the Cold Crush four with Tone a Chase
So come on Everybody in the party place

Caz Just throw your hands in the air
Uh. Uh.
Caz And wave em like you just dont care
Uh. Uh
Caz And if you're on the go cause we told you
so
All Somebody say ho! Ho
Ho, Ho   Ho, Ho,
Ho, Ho, Ho   Ho, Ho, Ho
And before you go

If, I'm the first and never last
All the ladies say Grand Master Caz.
Thank, Thank You

All You cant believe your eyes cause

Song The party's packed and jumpin
that funky bass is thumpin
and the way the music rocks your mind
ooh girl its really somethin

It's a place where you can dance
You can even find romance
And I know you can do it if you give yourself
a chance

All So just dance BREAK

Caz We're gonna let ya know
JD We're gonna let you see
JD What we're gonna do
Caz at the party

Grand Master Caz with looks to spare
I'm gonna chill with ladies when I get
there
You can call me Jerry D. or call me J.D.L.
and when I get to the jam, I'm gonna
rock it well.

④

89

And if Jerry D Lewis is too hard to spell
all the ladies say J.D.L
Thank, thank you

If all the young ladies can relate
to me, I wanna hear you say A.D.
thank, thank you

And if you're ready for the rythm
of the Almighty young ladies say Kay Gee
thank, thank you

If the four of us are really a must everybody
say Cold Crush, Cold Crush
thank, thank you   ECHO 3x's   BREAK

When the jam is over
CAZ You head for the stairs
All the girls and the fellas
JDL are leaving in pairs

You had such a good time
AD You wish you could stay
KG But now it's time to take the bus
train or
4 OJ

CAZ Then you get to your house
and pull out the key
Because your tired as hell
JDL You're gonna sleep to three

EAD Then you woke up Sunday
wipe the sleep from your eyes
AKG Go out into the sun for
some exercise

Play ball, roller skat or
visit a freind
Then go home and think about
The next weekend.

end

Furious Lovers

Mele Mel · Mr. Ness · Rahiem · Cowboy · Kid Creole
Introducing The Newest Addition

Whizkid

Wayne
Charlie

The Original "Water Bed - Kevie Kev"

Guaranteed to perform!
A DipLite & Bloodrock Prod.

Sat., Jan. 30, '82

Harlem World

Adm $6ºº

OR MONEY BACK

Buddy-Esquire

Jazzy Lee Productions PRESENTS

BUDDY·ESQUIRE'S

3RD ANNIVERSARY!

dj HOLLYWOOD

NEW YORK'S NO.1 UPCOMING

DYNAMIC FORCE

SEVILLE J SKI KELLY KEL STEPHANIE P

PERFORMING THEIR SOON TO BE RELEASED SINGLE

BREAKOUT

FUNKY 4

FRI. FEB. 26, '82

T*CONNECTION

GUYS $3 GALS $2 COUPLE $4

International Heavyweight Rapper Super Showdown

Easter Sunday

Fly Gi ls and Fly Guys Pr ,ctions Presents

For $1500
Winner Take All

Grand Master Flash
Also Performing Live On Stage

PAGES 96/101
*Here's a selection of Buddy Esquire's
original paste-ups for show flyers.
The design ideas are fresh, fly, and bold
to this day. His extreme attention to
detail and great talent for balanced,
eye-catching compositions combine an
Art Deco-influence (inspired by the
facades of the great crumbling Art-Deco
movie theatres that still existed in the
Bronx of the late 1970s) with a Star Wars
science-fiction vibe and a fondness for
classic Marvel comics.*

PAGE 108/109
*See here how Buddy Esquire cut
pieces out of Joe Conzo's photos for
incorporation into his flyers. Buddy and
Joe never met in person back in day,
only through their mutual work as
artists coming together. The two giants
of early hip hop art finally met in person
in 2004.*

PAGES 116/117
*Here's an opportunity to compare the
original paste-up with the printed flyer.
Buddy Esquire was meticulous in his
attention to detail, and would often make
blueline proofs of the flyers when they
were printed offset.*

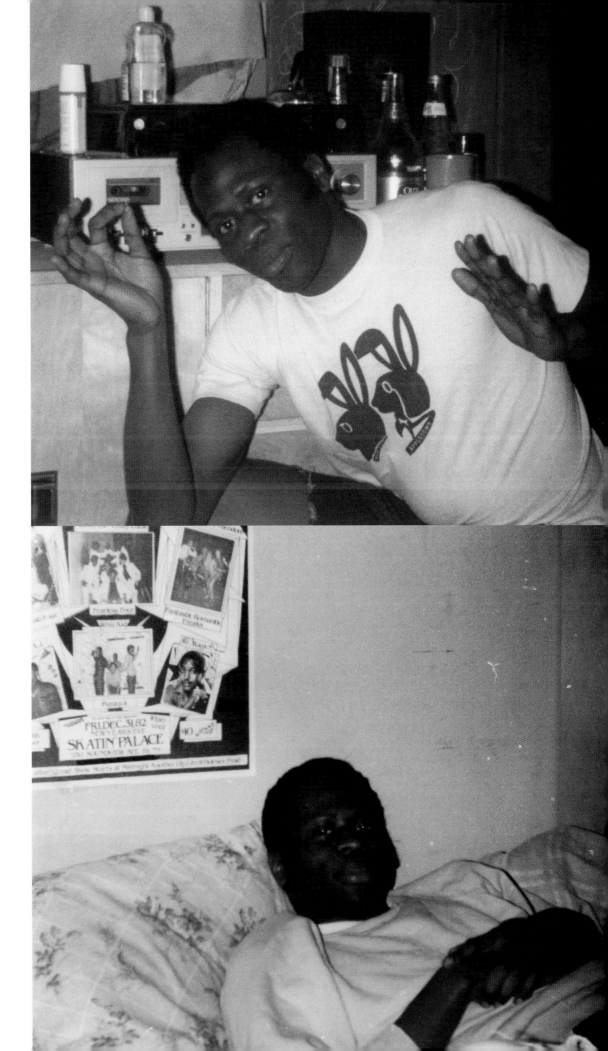

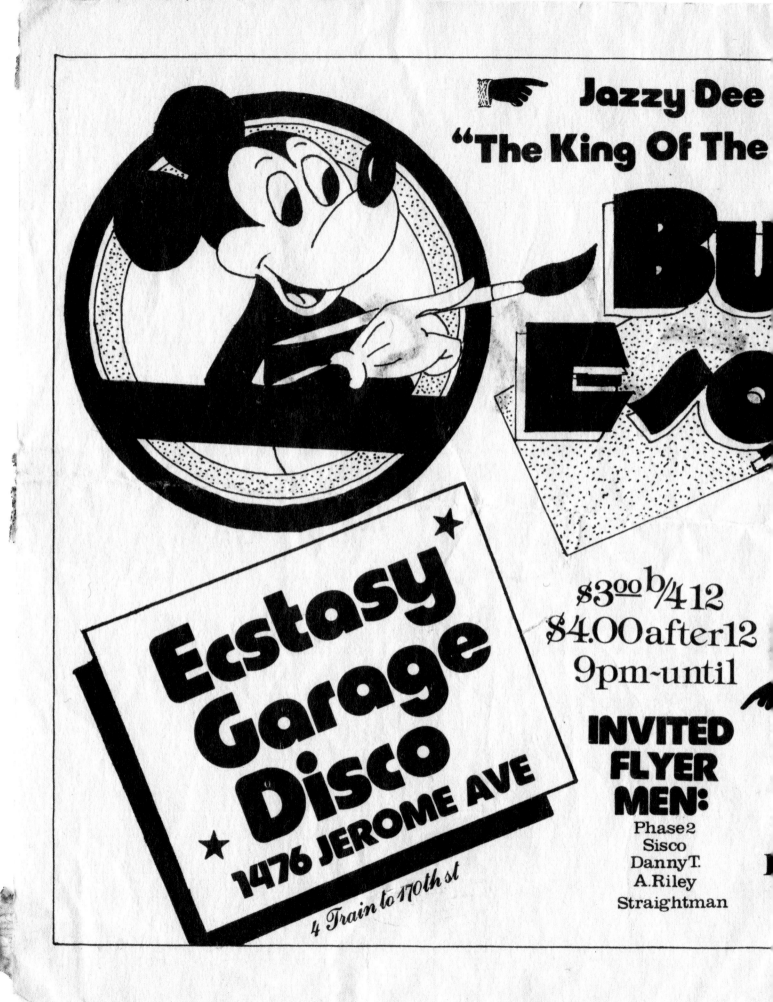

oductions presents a tribute to

yer" the man by the name of...

DDY

UIRE!

→ SAT.
Feb. 23,
'80

the BROTHERS
DISCO

DJ BREAKOUT   DJ BARON

The
nky4
isOne

Keith-Keith K.K.Rockwell
Sha-Rock Jazzy-Jeff
Lil-Rodney C

Buddy-Esq.. To Vega Ray

The T Connection

Dec. 25 Christmas Day

The Brothers Disco

Sisters Disco!

D.J. Breakout · D.J. Baron

The Funky 4 M.C.s
Sha-Rock · Keith-Keith ·
Rahiem · K.K. Rockwell ·

$100. 9 pm - until

Spank Ladies $3.00
Contest Gents $4.00

Future Date - Dec. 26 and 7

at the Monte Rey

DO DRESS...
NO SNEAKERS!

These are the eighties and it all

about C.C. - Cold Crush!!

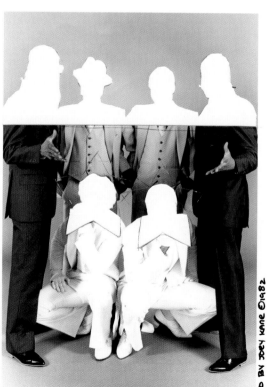

COLD CRUSH BROTHERS

Elite Recording Artist
P.O. BOX 23, N.Y.C. 10458

Ecstasy Garage Presents

A THURSDAY NIGHT OF FREE DISCO

◆ With House DJ's ◆

MEAN GENE
FANTASY 4 M.C.s

THE GRAND WIZARD THEODORE
FANTASTIC 5 M.C.s

Invited Guests

STARSKI **BAMBAATAA**
G.M. FLASH FURIOUS 5 M.C.s
BREAKOUT **BARON**
FUNKY 4 plus 1
G.M. CAZ JERRY-D
CHARLEY CHASE COLD CRUSH 4
THE HERCULORDS
PLAYERS DISCO TOUCH OF CLASS
ISLAM PETE DJ JONES

THURS, AUG. 28, 80

Ecstasy Garage Disco

1508 MACOMBS RD. 4,D TRAIN TO 170 ST. 10 PM-UNTIL

ECSTASY GARAGE

ADM. FREE!

WILL BE OPEN EVERY THURS, FRI, SAT

Buddy★Esq.★

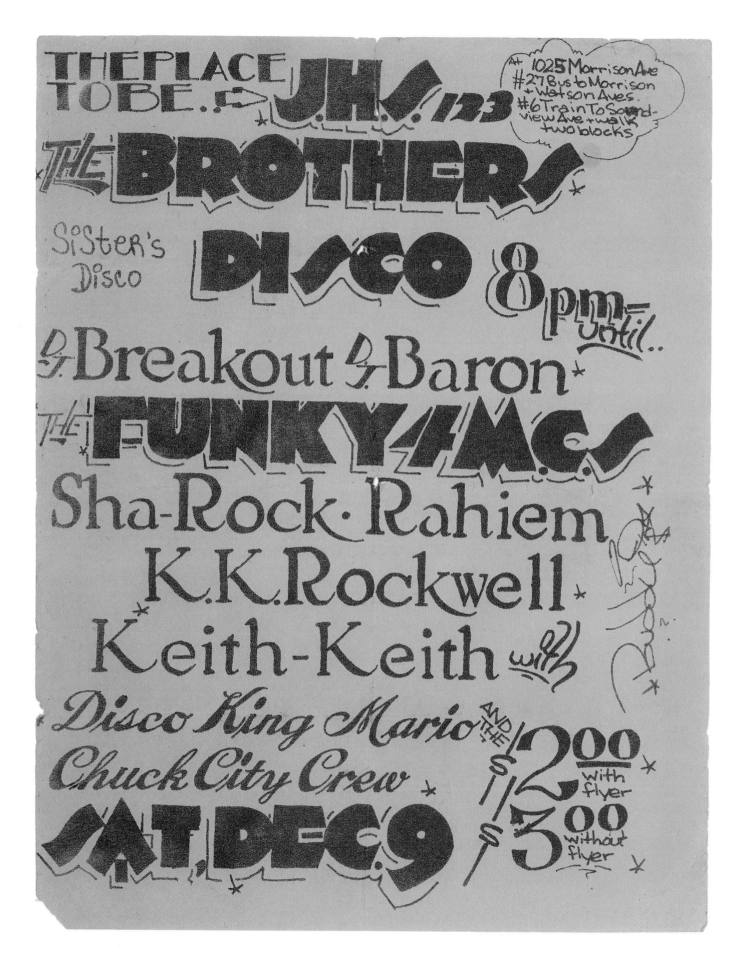

THE PLACE TO BE.. JHS 123

At 1025 Morrison Ave
#27 Bus to Morrison
+ Watson Aves.
#6 Train To Sound
view Ave + walk
two blocks

THE BROTHERS

Sister's Disco DISCO 8 pm - until..

DJ Breakout DJ Baron

THE FUNKY 4 MCs

Sha-Rock · Rahiem
K.K. Rockwell
Keith-Keith with

Buddy

Disco King Mario AND THE
Chuck City Crew
$2.00 with flyer
SAT, DEC 9 $3.00 without flyer

NUBIAN PRODUCTIONS PRESENTS
A Ladies Night
Free·Bee!
AT BRONX·RIVER·CENTER
1619 E 174 STREET
9 PM·UNTIL
SOULSONIC FUNK SOUNDS BY

D.J. Afrika...
BAMBAATAA Master of Records

The Original D.J.
JAZZY·JAY

SOULSONIC FORCEMC

Hutch·Hutch Ice·Ice
Pow·Wow Sundance
Lisa·Lee Master·Ice
Master·B

"THE NATION"
FRi. DEC 7 1979 9:00 AM. UNTIL ??

LADIES FREE BEFORE 12 AM
2.00 WITH FLYER AFTER 12
GENTS 3.00 ALL NIGHT

113

FEATURING **THE INCREDIBLE**
DJ BREAKOUT

&THE
Funky 4 plus-1-

KEITH·KEITH ★ K.K.ROCKWELL ★ SHA·ROCK ★ JAZZY·JEFF LIL RODNEY·C

PERFORMING
THEIR NEW HIT RECORDING
"THAT'S THE JOINT!"

Sat, Nov.1, 80

T ★ Connection
3510 WHT PLNS RD. 9PM-UNTIL
2 TRAIN TO GUNHILL RD.

To Cynthia

Adm ★ $3⁰⁰ b/4 12

Buddy Esquire

ECSTASY GARAGE PRESENTS
THE 1ST APPEARANCE EVER IN THE BRONX

SUPER RECORDING ARTIST

Super Rhymes
DOING HIS SMASH
"SUPER RHYMES RAP"

Also N.Y.'s No One MC
CHIEF ROCKER BUSY BEE
Starsky

WITH HOUSE DJ's
Mean Gene
FANTASY 4 M.C.s

SAT, SEPT. 13, 80

Ecstasy Garage Disco
1508 MACOMBS RD. 4, D TRAIN TO 170 ST. 10PM-UNTIL.

GUYS $5 GALS $4 til 12

SEPT. 11; GALS FREE til 12 GUYS $1

★ Buddy ★ Esq. ★

ECSTASY GARAGE PRESENTS
THE 1ST APPEARANCE EVER IN THE BRONX

SUPER RECORDING ARTIST
Super Rhymes
DOING HIS SMASH "SUPER RHYMES RAP"

Also N.Y.'s No One MC
CHIEFROCKER BUSY BEE
Starsky

WITH HOUSE DJ's
Mean Gene
FANTASY 4 M.C.s

SAT, SEPT.13,80
Ecstasy Garage Disco
1508 MACOMBS RD. 4, D TRAIN TO 170 ST. 10PM-UNTIL

 # GUYS $5 GALS $4 til 12

SEPT. 11; GALS FREE til 12 GUYS $1

★ Buddy ★ Esq. ★

117

Harlem World

PRESENTS

A Birthday Party For:

E·Z·A·D.

Coldcrush Brothers

CHARLIE CHASE   TONY·TONE

SUPERSTAGE SHOW BY

Coldcrush 4

SINGING
"CATCH THE BEAT"   SPECIAL ADDED ATTRACTION:

T·Ski Valley   Treacherous-3

FREE PHOTOS & POSTERS of the ColdCrush Bros.
ALSO A VIDEO TAPE SHOW BY TONY G.

Sat, Oct. 3, 81

9PM-UNTIL
$3 b·4 10:30
WITH FLYER

129·Lenox Ave. Wst. 116th St.

LOOK OUT FOR WEEKEND RAP BY COLDCRUSH BROS.

PHOTO BY: JOEY © 1981

Buddy-Esquire

2·3 116 ST

119

COLD CRUSH
BROTHERS

CHARLIE D.J. TONY~
D.J. CHASE TONE

COLD CRUSH 4
GRANDMASTER CAZ JERRY D. LEWIS
EASY A.D. KAY-GEE
& ESQUIRE TOO!

FRI, APR. 24, 81
BRONX
BOYS CLUB
1665 HOE AVE
31, 26 & 11 BUSES
2 & 5 TRAIN TO 174TH ST, WALK 2 BLOCKS

Ladies Gents
2⁵⁸
8-4/130

SOME TRACKS PLAYED BY CHARLIE CHASE IN THE WAY BACK WHEN

1.Meco — Star Wars **2.DC LaRue** — Indiscreet **3.Creative Source** — Who Is He and What Is He to You? **4. Manzel** — Space Funk **5.East Side Connection** — Frisco Disco **6. Yvette and the Kids** — Funky Drummer **7.Brothers Johnson** — Ain't We Funky Now **8.Melvyn Sparks** — Get Ya Some **9.Earth Wind and Fire** — Africano **10.Foster Sylvers** — Misdemeanor (instrumental version) **11.Isaac Hayes** — Pursuit of the Pimpmobile **12.Chuck Brown and the Soul Searchers** — Ashley's Roachclip **13.Chuck Brown and the Soul Searchers** — Bustin' Loose **14.E.U. Freeze** — Knock 'Em Out Sugar Ray **15.Edwyn Starr** — I Just Wanna Do My Thing **16.Dennis Coffey** — Son of Scorpio **17.Billy Joel** — Stiletto **18.Johnny Taylor** — Ever Ready **19.Johnny Hammond** — Shifting Gears **20.The Choice Four** — Come Down to Earth

TEN GREAT LIVE JAMS AND BATTLES

1.Cold Crush Brothers vs. Fantastic Romantic Five, Harlem World, 1981 The battle, the legend, and one of the most powerful recordings in all of hip hop's history. **2.Busy Bee vs. Kool Moe Dee, Harlem World, 1981** There were two battles: the first one, on Christmas Eve, was when the legend was made; Kool Moe Dee was unbelievable. Busy Bee got a re-match on New Year's Eve, which wasn't recorded. **3.Busy Bee, Grandmaster Caz, DJ AJ, and Grandwizzard Theodore, the Audubon, 1981** Busy Bee and Caz trading rhymes is a great thing, not to mention Theodore and AJ on top form. **4.Charlie Chase with the Furious Five, Forrest Projects, 1980** For a few weeks, Chase replaced Flash as the Furious Five's DJ after the Five and Flash had fallen out over money. Charlie Chase could certainly hold his own, and I rate him as highly as Grandmaster Flash. Why is evident on this tape. **5.Grandmaster Flash and the Furious Five, Bronx River Projects, c. 1978** Nobody knows the date for sure, but this was certainly where

Afrika Bambaataa's legendary plate was recorded. **6. MC Throwdown, Harlem World, 1982** A rare opportunity to hear T¿/Ski Valley perform. He performs his record "Catch the Beat" as well as some pretty amazing routines. The Cold Crush are brilliant as usual, and Spoonie Gee is in full effect. **7. The L Brothers vs. The Herculoids, T-Connection, 1978** Grandwizzard Theodore cuts like a fiend on this legendary recording. **8. DJ Grandmaster Flowers, park jam in Brooklyn, 1979** It's obvious why this DJ is such a hushed legend. A dubby performance with heavy echo and some extremely obscure (to this day!) disco breaks. **9. New Music Seminar Battle of the DJs, New York, 1982** Hosted by Grandmaster Caz, with performances on fire by Charlie Chase, Jazzy Jay, and Whiz Kid. **10. Masterdon and the Death Committee, Busy Bee, Cold Crush Brothers, and LA Sunshine, Harlem World, 1982** Crazy high-energy performances all round.

TEN 12-INCH MASTERPIECES OF EARLY RAP

1. Nice and Nasty 3 — The Ultimate Rap (Holiday Records, 1980) A true dare-you-to-sit-still classic and floor-filler to this day. **2. T/Ski Valley — Catch A Beat (Grand Groove, 1981)** Industrial strength groove and some jaw-dropping rhymes: everybody, "They heard of me in Germany." **3. Family — Family Rap (Sound of New York, 1979)** One of Steinski's favorite early hip hop tracks, and he is right as usual. **4. Masterdon Committee — Funk Box Party (Dee Jay, 1982)** Pebblee Poo, the great, underrated female MC, killing it. **5. MC Chocolate Star — Do The Pop (Chocolate Star, 1982)** Very strange and spooky early drum-machine track with a child MC. **6. Pookey Blow — Get Up (And Go To School) (Tri-State, 1983)** The 13-year-old MC blows minds over a beat so funky it was included on Volume 4 of the Octopus Breaks series. **7. Super 3 — When You're Standing On the Top (Street Beat, 1982)** A Cut Chemist favorite and a pull-you-up-by-yer-bootstraps party-rocker. **8. Fly Guy — Fly Guy Rap (Land of Hits, 1981)** Primitive and funky Peter Brown production with a swaggering, breathless Harlem rap on top. **9. Yella — Yella (Antilles, 1981)** Crazy, effect-smeared New York-centric take on "Genius of Love." **10. Spoonie Gee and the Treacherous Three — New Rap Language (Enjoy, 1980)** A masterpiece of fast rap.

(Fly guys, is-e-is-e the sure shot, sure shot?) Don't you know that The cheeba hawks is hawkin' (Hawk-hawkin') The stick-up kids are stalkin' (Stalk-stalkin') With the price of transportation now It's cheaper to be walkin' (Walk-walkin') 'Cause girls are just dick teasin' (Teasin') For no apparent reason (Re-reason) If fellas was to press treason They'd be in jail off-season (Off-season) So what ya gonna do? To stop captain 'n' the crew You got a hour or two Before the party is through (To stop captain 'n' the crew) Keep rockin' our beat ('Cause it sounds so sweet) Keep rockin' our beat (To-to the break of dawn, we gonna rock along) Now you heard of the Furious (Five) And you heard of the Fantastic 4 + 1 And I'm sure you know the Fantastic (We don't say that no more) And you know, Love Bug Starski And the Chief Rocker Busy Bee But these are the '80s And it's all about CC (Cold Crush) 'Cause we cold crush the parties (Pa-pa-ties) Make you wanna get down Cause we tellin' ya now We got a gallon of juice (Hey) The 4 is in your (The 4 is in your (The 4 is in your town) A rock shockin' around Yo, who that sound? A Charlie, a Charlie, a Charlie-wally-wally-wally-wally Chase never leavin' the girls alone And all the bass never leavin' Chase alone And Charlie Chase never leavin' the bass alone And all the bass never leavin' Chase alone And Tony Tone never leavin' the girls alone And all the girls never leavin' Tone alone (Leavin' Tone alone) Leavin' Tone alone Leavin' Tone alone Everybody say "one" (Uh-uh-uh-uh) One (Uh-uh-uh-uh) One (Uh-uh-uh-uh) One (Uh) Two (Uh) Two (Uh) Three, Four Hey ya'll Charlie Chase and the Cold Crush Four (Uno, dos, tres, quatro) Hey (Fly girls) Everybody Now, don't you know that (We got) Hey (We got) Hey (We got) Hey We got, we got, we got something new (And it's just for you) And it's just for you And it's just for you (And it's just for you) **AFRIKA BAMBAATAA, THE JAZZY 5 MCS, T-CONNECTION, 1981** So, listen everybody (Listen everybody) Listen up, everybody (Listen everybody) 'Cause we got a surprise (Got a surprise) Yes indeedy, New York City lookin' pretty, have no pity 'Cause I'm the Master Ice and I'm in your city, hey (Hey!) Now it's time to throw Go high and low and do the Gigolo Shake your body to the left (Shake your body to the right) Go down to the floor, now you're lookin' out of sight Then you come back up and look your partner in the eyes You'll find yourself headin' for a big surprise Because you split your pants a-when you went real low (And that's why we called it the Gigolo) Ha ha! (Gigolo, Gig-Gigolo, Gigolo) Serious, serious, c'mon I say clap your hands and do the Gigolo (Gigolo) (Clap your hands and do the Gigolo, Gigolo!) Listen party people all across the nation All we want from you (Is your co-operation) And if yo,u're gettin' down with no (Limitations) Everybody say "Jazzy Sensation!" (Jazzy Sensation) Jazzy Sensation! And you don't stop that body rock It's on, it's on, it's on (Yah ha haa!) And if you know the words why don't you sing along? Can you feel it? Can you feel it? Our Jazzy Sensation Zulu Nation, Zulu Nation (Aww shit) That's our creation **COLD CRUSH BROTHERS AND KURTIS BLOW, SKATING PALACE, 1982** People in the place, with the bass in your face You 'bout to see first place in the rap race The sounds that you hear So good to your ear Ya have no fear 'Cause Kurtis Blow is here And introducing the Disco Dream on the mean machine Darth Vader on the slide fader No one cuts straighter or greater Than New York's number one cut creator Goes by the name of Davey D Rocks so viciously From land to land, sea to sea With a Ph.D. 'n' Master's Degree And all that stuff that goes down in history And I am, Kurtis Blow Kurtis Blow is my name Rappin' is my game I'll do the playin,' you do the payin' Satisfaction guaranteed, you get no money back 'Cause I could never be the wack And that's why I talk shit like that **THE L BROTHERS VS. THE HERCULORDS, ZULU NATION, BUSY BEE, T-CONNECTION, 1978** Well, as I rock New York City all years round Hey, my name is known all over the town And the people here dig the way I run my game They can't wait to see me make the Hall of Fame Busy Bee is my name and that's a fact And as long as I'm rockin' ya'll I can never be the wac× Just take a little time, check out my style Don't need to brag because I'm versatile 'Cause I am the man with the master plan I got all the young ladies in my blue sedan As I tour the street all through the night To hang with me, you got to be alright Say winter, spring, summer, or fall Anytime you're ready you can gimme a call We'll talk about the birds 'n' the bees And the way I got my name, I'm Busy Bee Busy Bee is my name and ya'll well know You paid cash money to see this show So listen babydoll, while I pop this shit Ain't no fly girl Chief Rocker can't hit Uh-nah-shoo-bop-da-bop, say uh-Busy Bee on the rise 'Cause I'm MC Bust-A-Nut, ow In yo' face 'n' in yo' butt I'm MC Bust-A-Nut, ya'll, In yo' face 'n' in yo butt A through rain through shine Your house or mine Hip hop ya don't stop Say uh-ah-um-um-ah, fly girls don't stop until you reach the top Say ooh-ah-ooh-ooh-ah, fly girls don't stop until you reach the top I'm the B-U-S-Y-B-E-E And I'm not talkin' 'bout Muhammad Ali Watch me float like a butterfly, sting like a bee I'm the champ of the mic and they call me Busy Bee That we call Bronx River Center Featuring the girl we call the elegant DJ Wanda D on the wheels of steel And yours truly, the Queen MC Debbie Deb on the microphone And it's us, ya'll, with no fuss, ya'll And on the wheels of steel showin', you the real deal The girl we call the elegant DJ Wanda D And I am Queen MC, Debbie D, and I want ya'll to know that And just for all the ladies, we want ya'll to know that We are the ladies of the 80s it's us, ya'll, with no fuss, ya'll And take that, because we're not the wack And take that, ya'll, and rock shit, ya'll And take that, ya'll, we're not the wack, ya'll **CHARLIE D AND NICE & NASTY 3 VS. COLD CRUSH BROTHERS, T-CONNECTION, 1981** Now, some call me Charlie, some add the D No matter how you say it, I'm a def MC I got a ring on my finger that's made of solid gold I got grey hair, but I'm not that old Rockin' the beat I got so much pizzazz Down with the crew they call the Touch of Class A Touch of Class with the Nice & Nasty 3 Together we rock until eternity A young ladies rock the house A freak a funk to the beat, now watch me turn it out Well, I'm the C the H the A the R the L the I the E The ever lovin' boy, you can call me Charlie D Rockin' the house to the beat so funky You get up and dance like a disco monkey Rock the house to the beat always doin' the jazz While you listen to the rhythm of the razz-a-ma-tazz Gonna do it, gonna rock the rock Charlie D in the place and I'm gonna hit the top Like a this, ya'll, like a this, ya'll Because you know I'm on the top of the list, ya'll A hip hop ya'll, a hip hop ya'll 'Cause I never ever never never never wanna never stop, ya'll So? Ray, ha, it's at your own risk Pick up the mic, do whatcha like Pick up the mic, but don't you dare miss **PRINCE WHIPPER WHIP AND THE FANTASTIC FIVE, 1980** Because we here to give you all a demonstration All we ask for is cooperation Just clap ya hands everybody and everybody clap ya hands C'mon, just clap ya hands everybody and everybody clap ya hands And if you feel real high and ya ready to go Because what ya paid at the door was all your gusto If you asked a girl to dance, the girl said, "No" All the fellas in the house say, "Hooo" And to the ladies, young ladies, if ya ain't eatin' Cat Chow I want ya cooperation right now The niggas don't dance 'cause they don't know how So all the ladies in the house say, "Owww" And everybody, if ya make cash money and ya got it like that Everybody say and ya know that Because we're not the wack I say one, two, three, four Whatcha got for me, DJ Theodore? Well, I'm Prince Whipper Whip and I wanna be known As the professional magician on the microphone Two plus one is three, 'cause I'm here to rock for all the ladies Guaranteed to shock all the fellas, too Because I came here to rock for you 'n' your crew Check it out, huh, you don't stop So get ready to rock to the finger pop To the rhythm of the beat that makes ya body rock To the rhythm of the beat ya can't stop Don't stop that body rock, 'cause the beat-beat is always right on time Well, he's the Grandwizzard DJ Theodore There's one thing I never told you before That he can rock the mic, like the turntables Grandwizzard is ready, willing, 'n' able He'll cut a record here, cut a record there Slice 'n' dice with the mix everywhere Make all the freaks just stand 'n' stare And Fantastic Five, ya just best beware We here to rock, huh, ya don't stop So c'mon, Theodore, let's shock this spot Do it up right, let's do it good We're rock-shock-rock rollin' in ya neighborhood Rock, ya don't quit, 'cause I'm here to rock for you 'n' your crew, I can't quit 'cause I'm the Whip, you know I got to go on Because the music's got to be the shit The rhythm of the beat ya just can't quit Because ya bein' hypnotized by me, a Whipper Whip And that's the shit, ha ha, so get funky Young ladies, you know I can't quit 'Cause I'm the Whip, you know I got to go on Because I rock the funky rhythm to the break o'dawn Because I make the party people just rock it on Like a hippid-a-hop, say what, popcorn? So just clap ya hands everybody and everybody clap-clap-a-clap-clap-clap-clap-clap ya hands Prince Whipper Whip, I'll make ya understand the party people just rock it on Like a hippid-a-hop, throw ya hands in the air, When I pull my trigger and my gun go blow, young ladies in the house say, "Owwww" Now fellas, if ya got cash money and ya pullin' the hoes Scream it out and say, "Hooo" Ya don't stop, keep on with the body rock Grandmaster Caz won't you shock the spot So just throw ya hands in the air, throw ya hands in the air When I pull my trigger and my gun go blow Gonna rock the beat in ya neighborhood Everybody in the house if ya on the go, scream it out lemme hear ya say, "Hooo" Ya don't stop, keep on with the body "I got gusto" We're gonna do it up right, we're gonna do it good Gonna rock the beat in ya neighborhood Everybody in the house say the spot

KOOL MOE DEE VS. BUSY BEE STARSKI, HARLEM WORLD, 1981 One for the treble, two for the bass Come in Easy Lee and let's rock the place One-two one-two, doin' the do now Hold on, Busy Bee, I don't mean to be bold But put that bop diddy bop bullshit on hold We gonna get right down to the nitty-gritt Gonna tell you a lil' something, why you ain't the shit It ain't an MC jock that you don't hug You even bit your name from the Love Bug And now to bite a nigga's name Is a lowdown shame (Shut up, shut up!) If you was money, man you'd be counterfeit I gotta give it to you though, you can rock But everybody know you on the Furious jock And I remember Busy from the olden times When my man Spoonie Gee used to sell ya rhymes Remember that that rhyme called diddy bop diddy Man, goddamn, that shit was a pity Too hot to trot Here to rock the spot Spoonie Gee rock it whether you like it or not He begged for the rhyme, asked for it twice He said, "Spoonie Gee, I'll buy it any price" When Spoonie finally sold it, oh what a relief Busy Bee stole it like a fuckin' thief Came out rockin', the party charged (Shut up!) Got everybody thinkin' that that rhyme's yours Everytime I hear it, I throw a fit Party after record, rhyme after rhyme Always wanna know your zodiac sign He changed the shit to the favorite jean Come on, Busy Bee, tell me what that means Hold on, brother man don't ya say nothing I'm not number one, you're not even the best And you ain't got You're not finished yet, I gotta tell you something Too hot to trot I'm here to rock the spot I'm gonna rock your ass whether you like it or not I'll take your title right on the spot How can I take a title you ain't got? You're not number one, you're not the best And you can't say it like me But ya wanna be, biz ya wanna be And you know the kind of stuff everybody knows Celebrity clubs are those the kinds you can win It's all set up before we come in But in a battle like this, you know you'll lose Between me 'n' you, who do you think they'll choose? Well, if you search real hard I'm sure you will find Ain't another MC who can rhyme like this Not your mother or your father, aunt, brother, or your sis Sit back 'n' enjoy, don't try to bite 'Cause it's very hard to say any rhyme I write But uncle rock-the-house, ya'll Like this, ya'll, like this, ya'll Like this-a-this, it's like this, ya'll Now you popcorn peanut toy MCs Never ever ever heard no rhymes like these 'Cause my intent from the time I sent Is to say those rhymes wanna be another Kool Moe Dee So let's all chant because you can't Everybody salute to the new MC champ It's like this, ya'll, like this, ya'll Now that bop-diddy-bop-da-dang-da-dang-dang Sound pretty good, but it ain't no thang I'm the super-scooper-party-pooper **GRANDWIZZARD THEODORE AND THE FANTASTIC ROMANTIC FIVE, LIVE CONVENTION, BRONX, 1982** It's like a one for the treble and two for the bass Theodore, let's dog the place The highs were screamin' and the bass was shakin,' And it won't be long 'til everybody knows That Flash was on the beat box goin' That Flash was on the Beat Box goin' And, and, and, and Sha-na-na **GRANDMASTER FLASH AND THE FURIOUS FIVE, SKATING PALACE, 1982** It was a party night, everybody was breakin,' You don't stop, that body rock Just clap your hands, it's the sure shot sound Brace yourself for the one that goes down Got a little news that you all can tell Theodore, he got the clientele All night y'all, if it's all right All night y'all, if it's all right Puerto Rico, Puerto Rico Make money, make money, make money Into the Patty Duke Throw your hands in the air Wave 'em like you just don't care Getting down with these sure shot sounds Your body say "Oh yeah" Yeah, a little louder, little louder You don't stop, you won't, don't, don't You won't, don't, don't Stop the body rock Because the people in the back, you ain't the wack But don't stop that body rock The people in the middle, let me see you wiggle But don't you stop that body rock Young lady in the rear, you come up here But don't you stop that body rock Young lady in the blue, I am talking to you But don't you stop that body rock The people in the side, let us ride But don't you stop that body rock Young lady in the black, you ain't the wack You ain't thinking about stopping that body rock Young lady in the brown, you know you're down Don't stop that body rock Young lady in the green, you are looking real clean Don't you stop that body rock Young lady in the yellow, got a faggot for a fellow But don't you stop that body rock 'Cause the body rock is sure enough the sure shot But you won't stop, you don't stop Ain't thinking about stopping that body rock Young lady in the white, she'll bite all night But don't you stop that body rock Young lady in the blue, I am talking to you But don't you stop that body rock Young lady in the black, you ain't the wack You ain't thinking about stopping that body rock Young lady in the blue, I am talking to you But don't you stop that body rock

THE FURIOUS FIVE, CHARLIE CHASE, MELLE MEL AND THE MERCEDES LADIES, LOCATION UNKNOWN, 1981

COLD CRUSH BROTHERS VS. THE FANTASTIC FIVE, HARLEM WORLD, 1981

THE FANTASTIC FIVE, DJ CLARK KENT, KEVIE KEV, T-CONNECTION, 1980

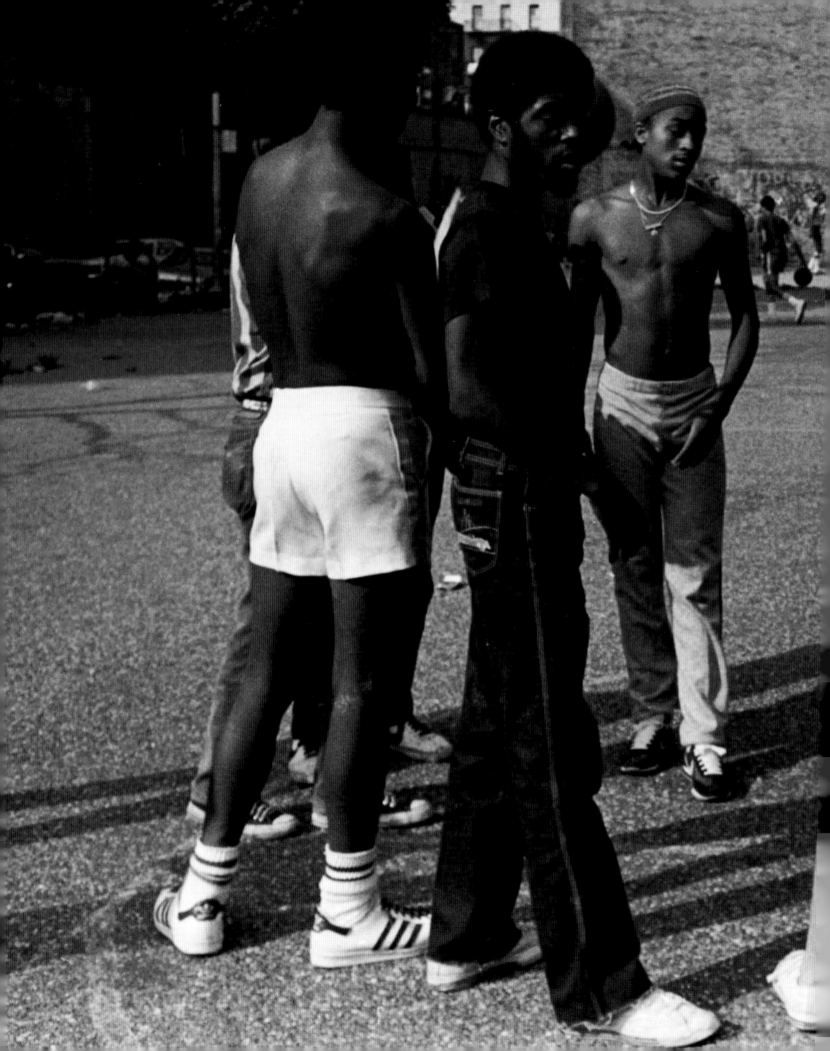

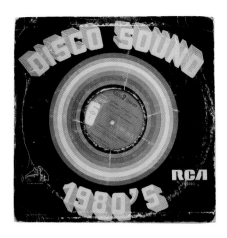

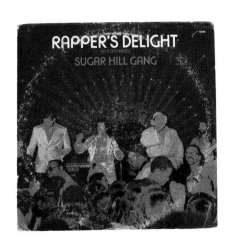
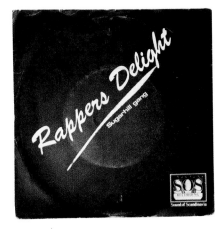

THE HUMBLE BEGINNINGS OF HIP HOP ON WAX

The many consecutive births of hip hop can be difficult to navigate for the neophyte and old-timer alike. Kool Herc brought the power of the Jamaican sound system to the Bronx, and with it the Jamaican MC moves of Coke La Rock that echoed back to King Stitt on the island, all of it now underwritten by the fattest of drum breaks courtesy of James Brown or the Incredible Bongo Band. After Herc discovered that the Bronx crowd would not listen to rocksteady and reggae, but instead to funk, soul, and Latin—and after being the first DJ to discover that the crowd would go truly apeshit over the break part of a record—he played those funk, soul, and Latin breaks over and over. Herc wasn't focusing on extending breaks with duplicate records, but his massive sound system was the first of its kind in the Bronx, playing funky records at breakneck volume and doing parties that were an alternative to the discos and nightclubs of Manhattan that wouldn't have let the b-boys and b-girls in anyway.

Grandmaster Flash was the first to extend the breaks. His original MCs Cowboy, Kid Creole, and Melle Mel took the shout-outs and catchphrases used by Coke La Rock and the radio-style announcements of DJ Hollywood, Pete DJ Jones, and Eddie Cheeba, and syncopated them to the beat, bouncing phrases between the three of them. The MC crew was born, and

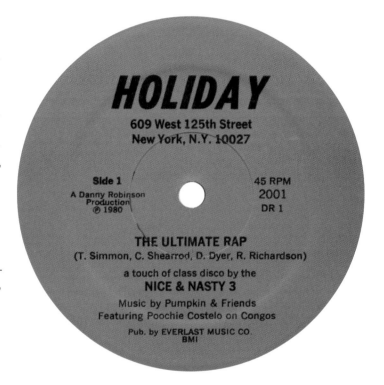

this invention spread like wildfire. Afrika Bambaataa, a member of the Black Spades and a renowned peacemaker and figure of authority among the gangs, was also a fanatical record collector with a knack for finding a funky beat in the most obscure of places. On November 12th, 1976, Bambaataa threw his first jam at the Bronx River Community Center. Countless were to follow, and the world changed for the better. Between Grandmaster Flash and Grandwizzard Theodore, the innovations of cutting and scratching were defined and refined, and music changed for the better. Before the blackout of July 14th, 1977, there were a handful of legitimate DJ crews spread across the Bronx. After the looting you had a DJ on every block.

The transition from a performance-based culture to a recorded culture (between 1978 and 1980) is a riddle wrapped inside an enigma stuffed inside a mystery hidden in a sock. The more you read, the more people you talk to, the more likely you are to run into contradictions. If you inquire about an event from two gentlemen who were there, each gentleman will remember the same event in completely different ways, and sometimes the same gentleman will remember the very same event in another four or five ways depending on his mood or who he speaks to. Not to mention those Grandmaster Caz refers to as the "lie-oneers" of hip hop: there are guys walking around uptown

taking credit for what other people did. What are you going to do? It isn't all that unlike the Kennedy assassination conspiracy when you think about it. Zapruders and grassy knolls are all over the place in the history of early hip hop, and it sometimes seems as if the old-timer old-schoolers have pitched tents and called the grassy knoll their permanent conspiratorial home.

In its transition from performed to recorded music, rap landed in the lap of the lowest common denominator: novelty music culture. After the mega-success of "Rappers Delight" (and in some instances before!), every swinging dick with the means to release an independent record and get it distributed jumped on the bandwagon, treating the music with the same finesse that ham-fisted opportunists of yore had handled the Twist or songs about flying saucers. Santa Rap. Sexy Rap. Baseball Rap. Pizza Rap. Party Rap. Out of

this came a lot of really shitty rap records—and, against all odds, some truly great ones. Sometimes great performers from the community ended up on record, but mostly some arbitrary guy or girl was dragged in who had never stepped up to a microphone before.

When you listen to the very earliest hip hop records—the 40 or 45 records that came out in 1979, the 200 or so that came out in 1980—most of the records are bandwagonesque, jumping on the craze as quickly as possible, getting something out as quickly as possible to cash in as quickly as possible. Certainly, originators such as Grandmaster Flash and the Furious Five come out on record, but for every one good record there'd be ten records of radio DJs rapping to a disco track, or novelty artists asking you to "Take My Rap, Please."

Those few months before "Rapper's Delight" was released in the autumn of 1979 saw a variety of records containing early attempts at rap. Small companies flinging tracks against the wall attempting to find a side that sticks. "King Tim Personality Jock" by the Fatback Band is commonly and incorrectly listed as the very first rap record. Scholar Freddie Fresh claims that Paul Winley released "Vicious Rap" before that, and we have seen evidence that the Baya Latinos record came out early 1979. There are cases to be made for another couple of the records you see before you as having been the very first one: contenders include Kebec Star, Tanya and Paulette Winley, First Choice, Dr. Superman and Lady Sweet or Bramsam. The people who released these records didn't keep archives or files or make discographies with an eye toward

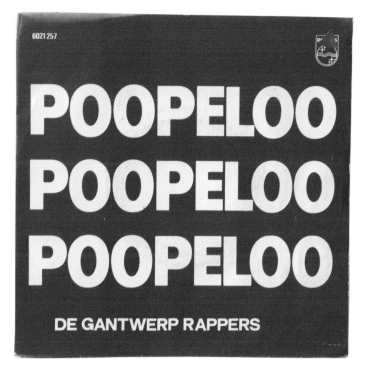

posterity and a place in pop-culture history. It is a fumble in the dark, finding out about this stuff, and the answer to the question "what was the first rap record?" is not an easy one to answer. Most people have never heard of most of these records, and that was as true back then as it is now.

The one that was the first to get stuck on the collective mind of the five boroughs (and then the world) was the Sugarhill Gang doing sixteen minutes of "Rappers Delight." Sylvia Robinson of Sugarhill Records had the epiphany that rap on record could get on the radio and could sell, really sell. After asking her son to bring her some MCs, he found her three marginal scenesters who recorded sixteen minutes of rhymes. The result swept the East Coast in the late fall of 1979 and became the kind of hit record that is unstoppable.

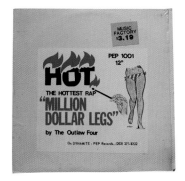

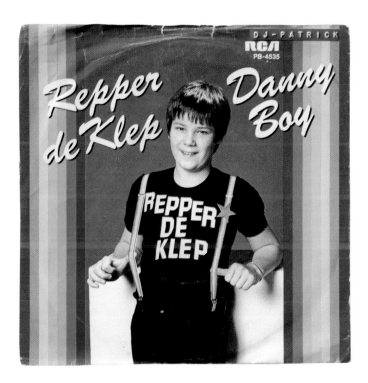

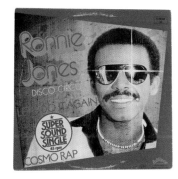

The mass market gobbled it up, in the same way that black R&B originators who didn't have hits back in the 1950s saw cover versions of their songs become hits in the decades that followed. It is possibly a necessity of the mass market that its first success belongs to the imitation rather than the originator. As always, the people who document the baby steps of a cultural force are the cunning businessmen, looking for novelty and a quick buck. Sometimes on purpose, sometimes by accident, they become the men and women who facilitate the existence of the artifacts that scholars argue about a few decades later.

The explosive, volcanic way in which "Rappers Delight" conquered the airwaves in the autumn and winter of 1979 has to be seen as a novelty

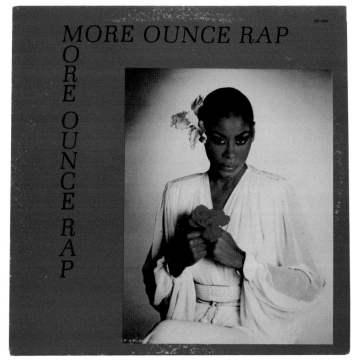

success. It can be compared with the Twist, or the Macarena, or "Crazy Frog," or any other more or less tedious tune that seduces the imagination of the masses. From the original pressing (red label and generic sleeve—the classic Sugar Hill Records graphics didn't exist yet) via overseas versions from Sweden, Venezuela, Germany, England, France, Mexico, Spain, Australia, Argentina, Brazil, and Uruguay, the world could not get enough of the grand groove, courtesy of master drummer Pumpkin and the Sugarhill session players re-constructing the Chic hit "Good Times," with lyrics that Big Bank Hank had stolen (or borrowed) from Grandmaster Caz of Cold Crush Brothers fame.

As the snowball effect took place, more labels appeared, more records appeared, and soon white people got hip to what was going on. Chris Stein and Debbie Harry of Blondie, in classic New York hipster mold, recognized something that was amazing, vital, and significant. Hosting *Saturday Night Live* in February 1981, they invited the Fantastic Four plus 1, whose performance on the show marked the first time a rap group had appeared on national television. Blondie's subsequent 1981 hip hop homage "Rapture" was certainly the first rap record heard by most white people, and much more of an international hit record than "Rappers Delight." It got ugly pretty quick, as it often does in the wake of a novelty hit. There are countless cheesy novelty rap singles from all over the globe between 1980 and 1982. Some are straight cover versions of "Rappers Delight" done in the local tongue; some are dismissive and seemingly jealous in a manner that reeks of imperialist racism; some are so idiotic that the mind boggles; and some are super-swinging

KURTIS BLOW

mercury

MANUFACTURED AND MARKETED BY PHONOGRAM, INC., A POLYGRAM COMPANY, 810 7TH AVENUE, NEW YORK, NY 10019 • DISTRIBUTED BY POLYGRAM DISTRIBUTION, INC.

MDS 4009
(MDS-4009-B)
SIDE B
8196 813

STEREO
33⅓ RPM

"RAPPIN' BLOW" – 7:58
(DO IT YOURSELF VERSION-INSTRUMENTAL)
(J. Moore/D. Miller/L. Smith/
R. Ford/K. Walker)
Previously Released As
"Christmas Rappin'" Dec. 1979.

Produced by J.B. Moore and
Robert Ford Jr. For Prep/Street
Productions
℗ 1979 Phonogram, Inc.

PRISM

I RAN IRAN

PDS 403
Side A
Time: 7:16
STEREO

33 1/3 RPM
DISCO SINGLE
℗ & © 1979
Prism Records, Inc.

DAVID LAMPELL
(David Lampell)

Published by: Malted Milk Music/Clarence
Lawton Music, ASCAP
Music Arranged by: Carl Maultsby/Maltese Falcon
Produced by: Clarence Lawton

FUNKY
Constellation

STREET-TALK
(Madam Rapper)
T. Osaze, W. Dixon, A. Mashaa
INSTRUMENTAL

#369
Produced by
Ted Osaze
and the Apostle
Eng.
Claude Watts
Quadrasonic Studio

33 1/3 RPM
STEREO

RENE.
by

The Funky Constellation
© 1979
Published by Frozen Butterfly Music Pub.

MACHINE RECORDS

45 r.p.m.
MR 1001

LADO 2
SADAIC
AADI-CAPIF
1981
Industria Argentina

PINO D'ANGIO
(Intérprete)

MA QUALE IDEA (pero cual idea)
G. Chercha - Pino D'Angio
Producido y Distribuido por MACHINE RECORDS

Reservados todos los derechos del productor fonográfico
y de los autores de las obras registradas en este disco.
Prohibida su reproducción, ejecución pública y/o
radioteledifusión.

NEWTROIT
Records

SIDE A
Stereo 33⅓ RPM
Time: (9:58)
(Intro) :19

NT-1001-A
© ℗ 1980
SPYDO-MUSIC
(BMI)

SPYDER-D
BIG APPLE RAPPIN'
(National Rappin' Anthem)
D. Hughes, E. Rice, R. Pierce
W. White, B. Motley

Prod. & Art by DUANE HUGHES
Co-Producer: TITO LEWIS
Exec. Producer: DORIS HUGHES

Manuf'd & Dist. by
LARCHWOOD MUSIC CO.
Woodbury Falls, New York 10950
(914) 551-0888

*TEST PRESSING
To Mr. Magic
of
WHBI 106 FM.
(EXCLUSIVE)
HAPPY BIRTHDAY
GRAND MASTER FLASH
+
The FURIOUS 5
JAN. 10, 1980*

classics of the art form! To hear which is which (Mae West voice), come up and see me DJ sometime.

And the art form evolves. With the success of Run DMC, the South Bronx performance-based roots of hip hop started to become dilapidated, the music changed, the drum machine became king and the breakbeat took the back seat, until the mighty Eric B and Rakim brought it back again. But that is another story.

J.K.

'Twas a night for rappers

By COLLIS DAVIS

To the "Rapper's De-light," whether one speaks of the Sugarhill Gang's re-cording success or the ta-lented thousands in the street, "Hiphop Talk" has rapped its way into the subconsciousness of black-ness. The rapping rage has reached such a virtuosic pitch that promoter Alton Chase got the brilliant idea of staging a City-Wide Rapper's Contest (Part I) at the Savoy Manor in the Bronx.

Sponsored by the Lincoln Republican Club, the show saw an enthusiastic turnout of contestants and fans alike. There were 17 solo and seven group entrants vying a shot at the winner-take-all $1,000 prize to be awarded in the March finals. Look for their an-nouncement in these pages for time and place of the climax event.

Informed "Hiphop Talknologists" gave Grand Master Flash and the Furious Five, who current-ly have an album at #8 on the charts, the nod for rhyming originality, but they may come under serious challenge from others in the running, now that they know what the real level of the rap is.

As for the origins of "hiphop," Chase credited a local, D.J. Hollywood, with its development before it was commercially record-ed.

Judges for Part I of the contest included local D.J.'s and non-partisan community people: D.J. Cisco, Melani, Leland El-Amin Shabazz, Lucenia, Jazzy Cynthia, Jesse Lynch, Africa Bambatta, and Timothy waitters. DJ-AJ was the guest D.J. of the night.

Promoter Alton Chase is also District Leader of the 76th Assembly District, Chairman of the Planning Board, and heads the secu-rity unit at River Park Towers.

Noted rapper Busy Bee Starsky verbalizes in syncopated phraseology prior to the start of the first City-Wide Rapper's Contest.

Rapper royalty, Grand Master (Bot., c.) and the Furious Five strike their winning pose backstage at Savoy Manor, Bx. The Five include Mele-Mel, Kidcreole, Mr. Ness, Cowboy and Rahiem.

Two camp followers seen at Rapper's Contest. Miss Erlyn Rodriguez and Tyrone Ford. (Collis Davis photos).

PAL PRODS'®

BOUNCE SKATE&ROCK ALL
NIGHT With

SPOONIE GEE

CHARLIE CHASE
and CREW

THEODORE
and CREW

PETE d.j. JONES

KOOL KYLE
&DiscoDolls

dj Sinbad

Sat. FEB 9,1980 9pm until?

Ladies $3
Gents $4

Come to the PAL at 183d and Webster Ave. Bx. N.Y.

Danny F

THE MONTEREY
Friday, August 8th

8 Shades of BLACK

BAND

* WITH DISCO MUSIC BY *

THE FORGIVE V5

DATE: FRIDAY, AUGUST 8. 1980

TIME: 9:00 pm. - UNTIL ???

PLACE: CLUB MONTEREY'S CALYPSO ROOM

4069 BRONXWOOD AVENUE (CORNER 229 th)

DIRECTIONS: TAKE #2 TRAIN TO 225 th ST.

PRICE: $3.00 PER PERSON

$5.00 PER COUPLE

(DRESS TO IMPRESS)

(NO SNEAKERS OR BROWN BAGS)

★ HIGH-SC

starring the:

RAPPERTEERS

With
D.J. 'MR. ICE'

ROYAL RAPPER
"DESIRE"

↓
RAPMASTER MELLOW-MELL &

also
Brooklyn's Baddest
KENNY GREEN
THE AWESOME 4 M.C's

APR 10 1981

chez-julie
221-24 LINDEN B

April

TIME - 9:00 P.M. until

OCIETY ★★
ODYSSEY

With
Rudy "B" &
D.J. Dee
The CMC Crew

Starring:

THE 'LIVING LEGEND' CASPER MIX MASTER FROM the BRONX

MR. JEE THE QUEENS-SHocker

$ MoNEY - "Σ" (BROOKIYNS-BEST)

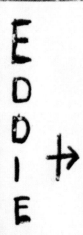

EDDIE →

Rappermatical 5

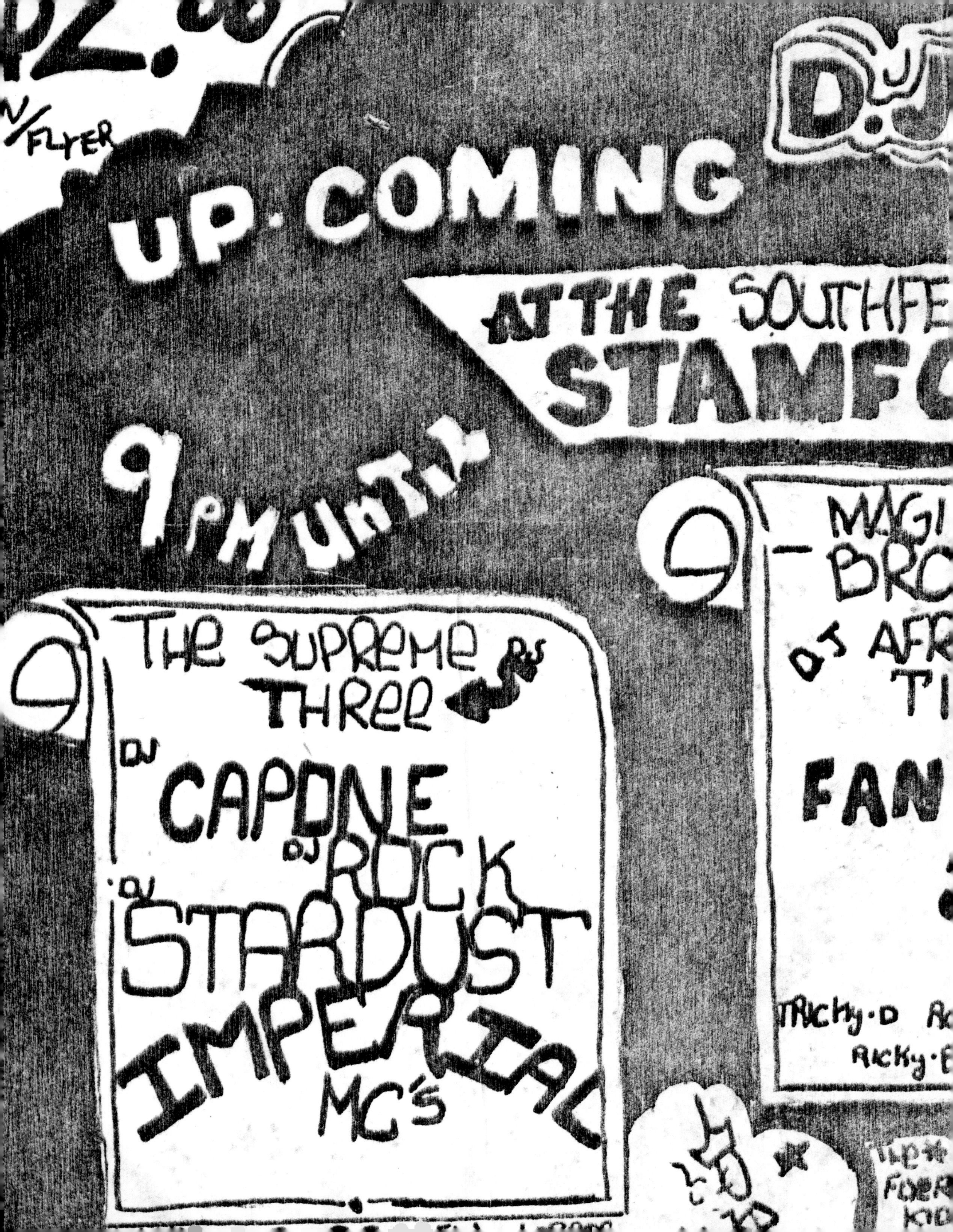

$2.00

w/FLYER

D.J.

UP·COMING

AT THE SOUTHFE
STAMFO

9 PM UNTIL

MAGI
-BRO

DJ AFR
TI

THE SUPREME
THREE

CAPONE
DJ ROCK
DJ STARDUST
IMPERIAL
MC's

FAN

TRICKY·D R
RICKY·B

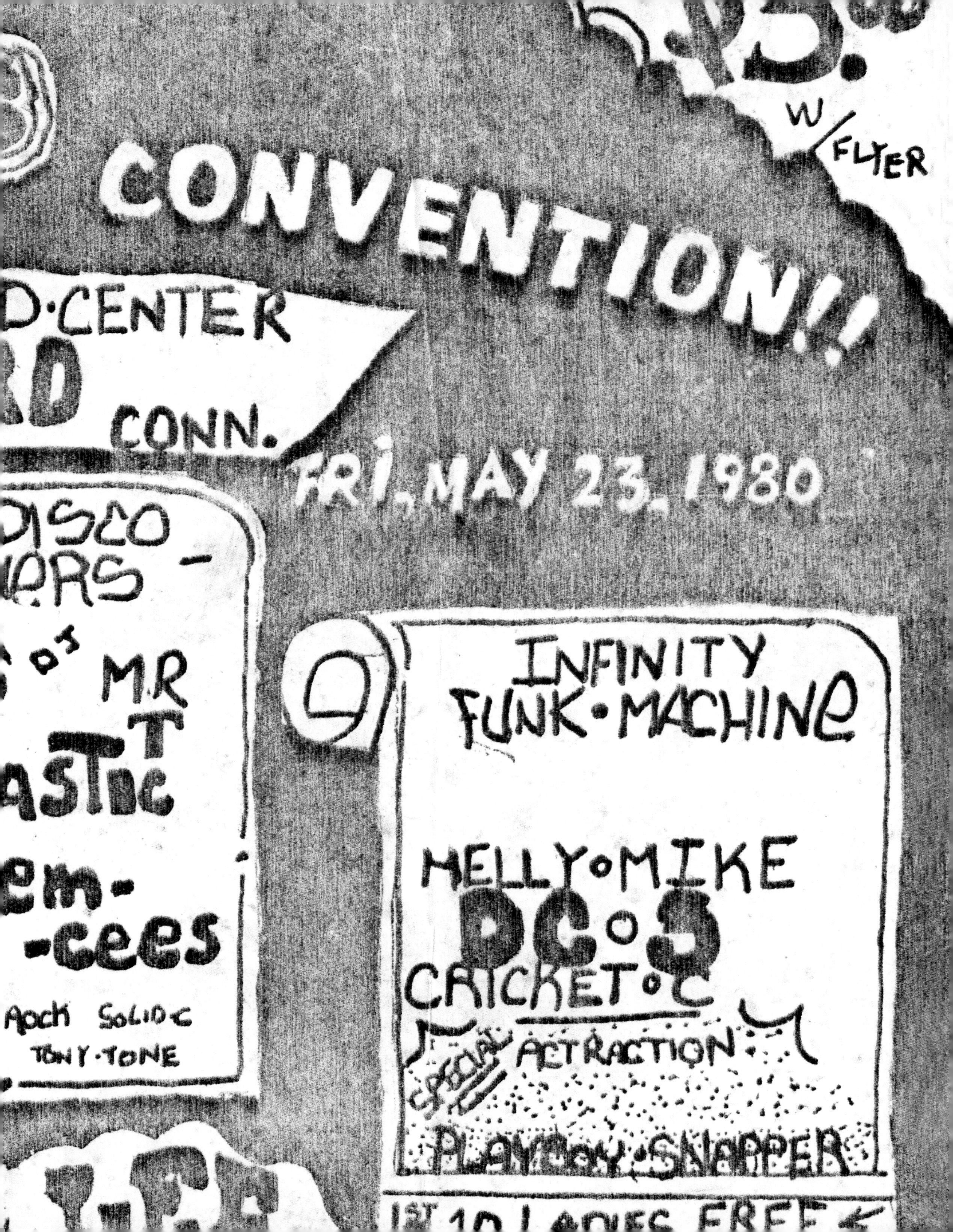

CONVENTION!!

$3.
$3.
W/FLYER

...D·CENTER
...RD
...RD CONN.

FRI, MAY 23, 1980

...DISCO
...IORS—
...S OT
MR
...T
T
...ASTIC
...em—
—cees
Apch Solid·c
TONY·TONE

INFINITY
FUNK·MACHINE

HELLY·MIKE
DC·3
CRICKET·C

SPECIAL ATTRACTION

PLAYBOY·SNAPPER

1ST 10 LADIES FREE

Come Celebrate The New Year!

with

JAMAICA'S QUEENS'S NO. 1 PERFORMERS

THE RAPPERMATICAL

| MELLOW GOO | TEE-SKI | CHUCKIE | CHILLIE-C |

DOING THEIR HIGH POWER DANCE SHOW

Also Featuring:

THE CLIENTELL BROTHERS

Eddie Ojay • Mr. Gene • Will-Seville • Easy-E

THE INCREDIBLE THREE EMCEE'S

DISCO VEE on the Funky Rhythm Machine

Special Guest:
RAPPER RON

Sound Apply by
T-PRODUCTION CREW

at the Beautiful "FAMILY"
224-13 Linden Boulevard
Take Q4 225 Street Linden and Walk One Block Down

JANUARY 2nd, 1982   FROM 9:00 - UNTIL
$3.00 WITH FLYER   NO SNEAKERS

The Best dressed Fly girl in the house will receive $50.00
This contest is judged by the Party People.

WARNING:
THIS JAM WILL BE UNDER
HEAVY SECURITY.

ROCK
W

LONVE
IN
PEACE

tation

Lil.
Brothers
Disco

Place: Hudson Giles Center
Address: 26 st between 8-9 Ave
Date: Fri. April 18, 80
Time: 9:00 PM - until

Cost For Repairs

$1.50 with Flyer $2.00
2.00 with out Without

666 West 125th St.

Presents **THE BEST M.C.ING POWER IN THE UNIVERSE!**

TOUCH OF CLASS DISCO

NICE & NASTY M.C.S

MEXI·RAY TERRY·TEE CHARLIE·DEE dj MELLOW·BEAT

ALSO NEW YORK'S NO.1 DANCE ORGANIZATION THE

Dance Masters
Psycho Eldarado Bruce

FRI.OCT.16,81

GUYS $5 GALS $4
BEFORE 12
$6 AFTER 12

All well known M.C.s are invited to

COLDCRUSH BROS. FANTASTIC 5
& UPCOMING D.J. PROTEGE.IKE!

Dance Master Psycho

INVITED GUESTS

BOOGIE BOYS MR MAGIC T·SKI VALLEY FORCE OF THE FIVE MC.S MERCEDES LADIES

BRONX	MAN.	BROOKLYN	QUEENS
THEODORE	LOVE-BUG	FRANKIE DEE	DIVINE
KOOL HERC	DONALD DEE	FLOWERS	DISCO TWINS
BAMBAATA	RONNIE GREEN	SPINDERELLA	CIPER SOUNDS
BREAKOUT	AL B	MASTER D	EASY AL
BARON	B-FATS	NUTCRACKER	KING CHARLES
FLASH	SPIVEY	FANTASIA	INNER CITY DJS
KOOL DJAJ	HOLLYWOOD		
ISLAM	DJ SMALLS		
ROCKIN ROB	SIR GAMBLE	STATEN ISLAND	INVITED MCS
CHARLIE CHASE	TEE JAY		
MEAN GENE	WHITE FLASH	DJ HINES	SPOONY GEE
SINBAD	KID FLASH	KOOL DJ JONES	FUNKY FOUR + 1
DJ GORDAN	DJ LEE	DR. FREAK	RAYVON
TOUCH OF CLASS DJ'S	CRASH CREW DJ'S	DISCO WIZ	GM. CAZZ
PETE DJ JONES	MAGNIFICANT 7	PARTY DOCTERS	WOODYWOOD
CLARK KENT	DJ GANGSTER		EDDIE CHEBA
"JC"			KURTIS BLOW
JAZZY JAY			

Dedicated to:

NORMAN THOMAS MANHATTAN VOC. MURRY BERGTRUM MUSIC & ART FASHION SATILITE H.S.

BRANDEIS HARLEM PREP MANHATTAN T TECH

All students with H.S.- I.D. & flyer - $1.00 off.

Plus the 'see it to believe it' sound system by Omar, Islam & Superman.

125th ST.

DARRell - Mount Vernon H.S.   URSellA
Delone - Spellman   My School
Burkes - Tolentine   Satelite
                           CHARLie Lit ALL
DAle - Stevenson   125st Stores Records
ARnold - Clinton
JAY - EVender   Norman Thomas
ROSS - TRUMAN   Bill-] Queens

-Tee - Corect   Jeff - BARUche College
HARlem World   Diso Fever
Mount St Micheal   ~~BOTA~~
Katharines

                           CRAZy Eddies - Fordhan Road
                           WAYne - Night School Roosevelt

652-5783

                    DEBBOE
                    409-2806

                                              #1 TRAIN to 125st
UANESSA
538-6940

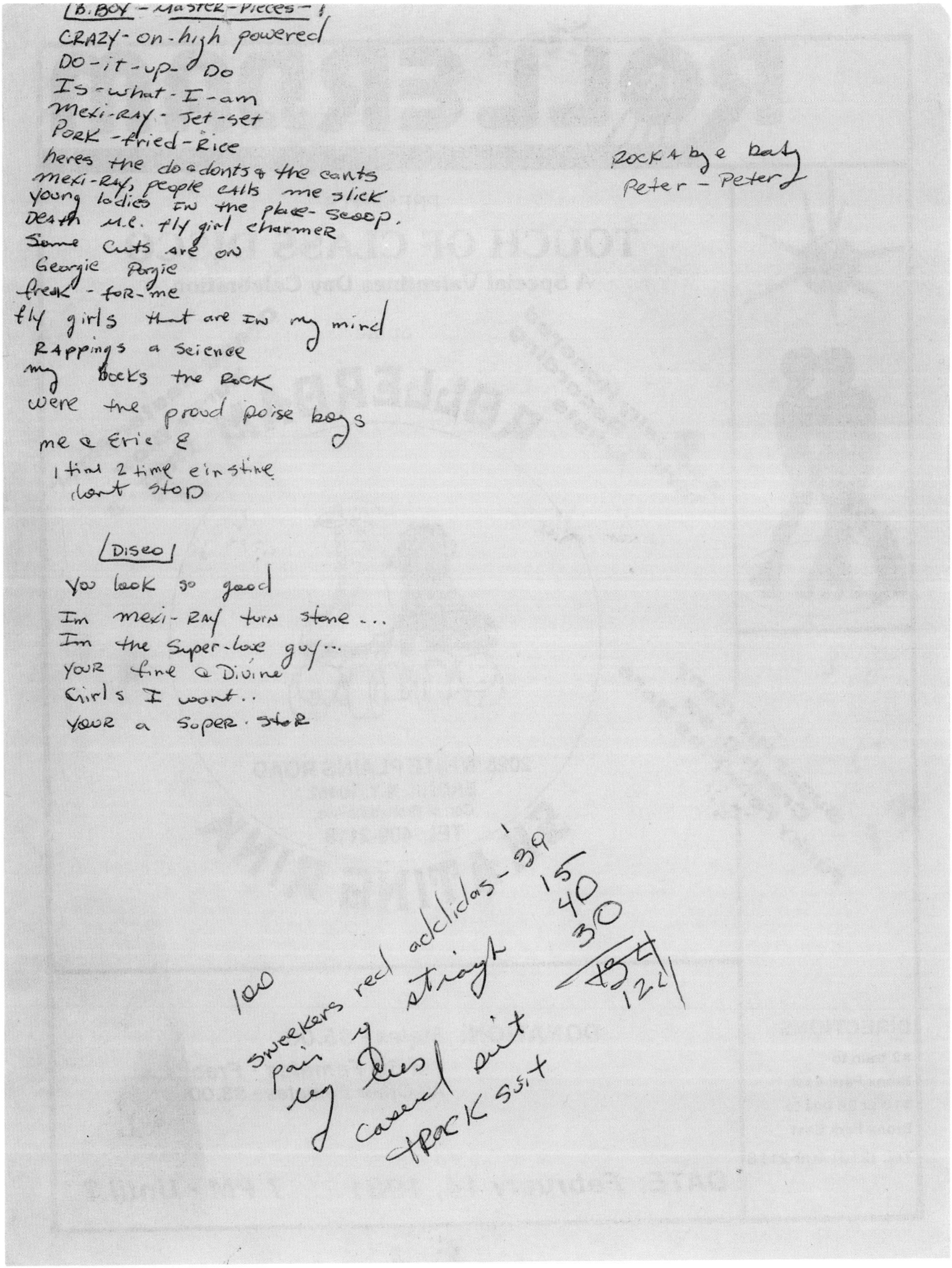

| B.BOY - MASTER - PIECES - |

CRAZY - on - high powered
DO - it - up - DO
Is - what - I - am
Mexi-Ray - Jet-set
PORK - fried - Rice
heres the do & donts & the cants
Mexi-Ray, people calls me slick
young ladies in the place - scoop
Death M.C. fly girl charmer
Some cuts are on
Georgie Porgie
freak - for - me
fly girls that are in my mind
Rappings a science
my docks the Rock
were the proud poise boys
me & Eric G
1 time 2 time einstine
don't stop

Rock a bye baby
Peter - Peter

| Disco |

You look so good
Im mexi-ray turn stone...
Im the Super-lov guy...
your fine & Divine
Girls I wont..
your a super-star

100
sweekers red adidas-39   15
pair y striagt   40
leg dus   30
casual suit   122
track ssit

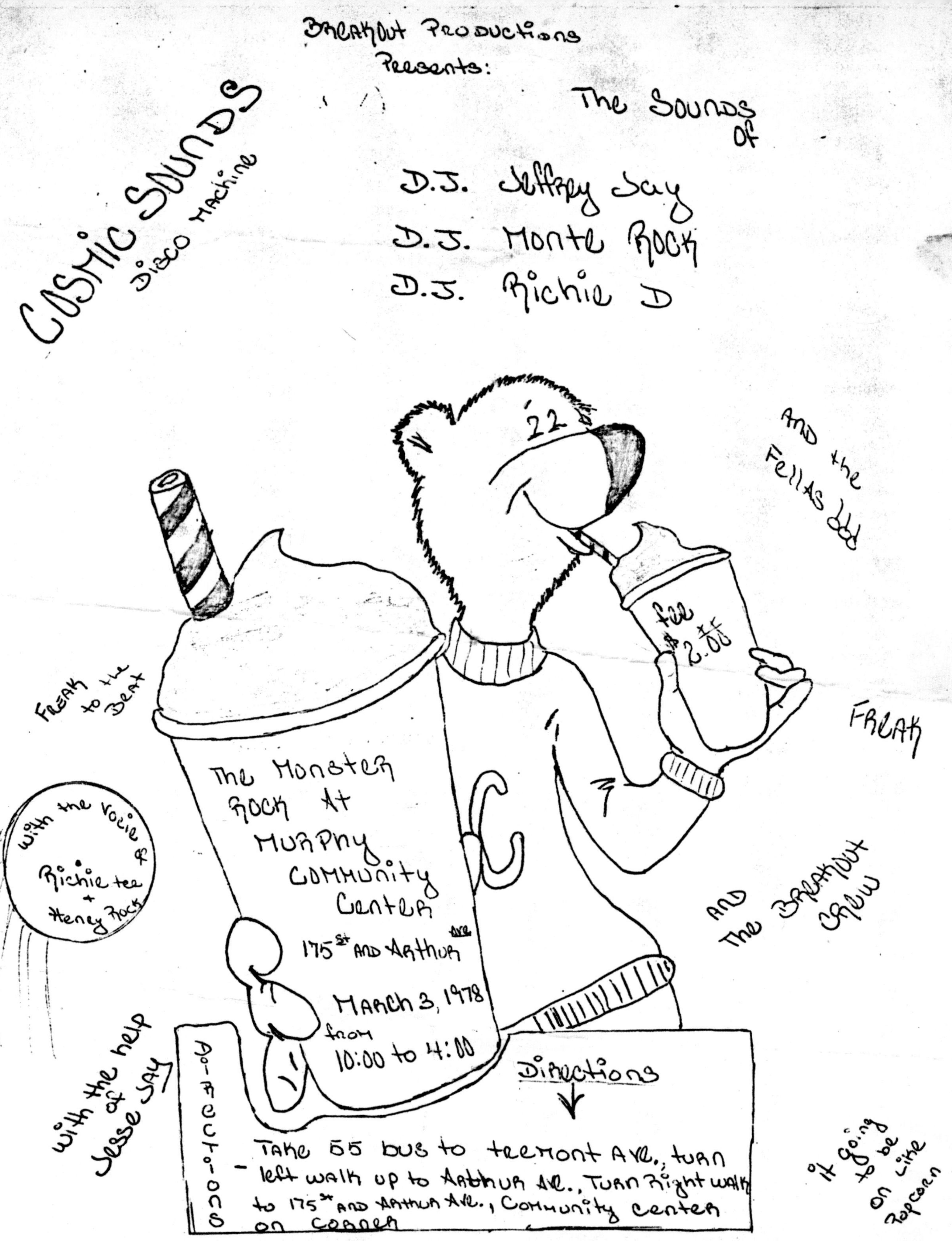

Breakout Productions
Presents:
The Sounds of
D.J. Jeffrey Jay
D.J. Monte Rock
D.J. Richie D
Cosmic Sounds
Disco Machine
22
And the Fellas
fee $2.00
Freak to the Beat
Freak
The Monster Rock At Murphy Community Center
175st and Arthur Ave
March 3, 1978
from 10:00 to 4:00
with the Vocie of Richie tee + Heney Rock
And The Breakout Crew
with the help of Jesse Jay
Directions
Take 55 bus to tremont Ave., turn left walk up to Arthur Ave., Turn Right walk to 175st and Arthur Ave., Community center on corner
it going to be on like Popcorn

K. Connection Presents A
Boss Sure Shot
Featuring

THE GRAND
IMPERIAL **KENNY·KEN**
DEE·JAY

Coach Doc La Rock
Three's Company
E·Z Mike

THE
GIRL **Paradise**
M.C.

Kid·Shadow

Special Guest
G.M. **Caz** AND **Jerry D** Lewis
Fri. Nov. 28, 80 7:00 UNTIL
$3.00 AFTER 11:00
1ST 25 Ladies
LADIES $1.00 B/4 11:00 FREE
James Monroe COMMUNITY
MEN $2.00 Center 1780 Story Ave.
BEFORE 11:00 * 27,5,54 BUSES TO MONROE HOUSES
ANOTHER ⇛ⅉ☀⇛ 1980 FLYER PRODUCTION Don't Come Wrong

COME In Peace

♦THOMPSON♦ TO ♦MILLIE♦MILL

A LOST TIME

Joe Conzo

The 1970s are a lost time. Demonstrations and protests were my playground growing up. My grandmother, Dr. Evelina Antonetty, started a Parent/Teachers Organization, and was instrumental in introducing bilingual education into the public schools. She was instrumental in feeding the homeless back in the '70s when they started the summer lunch programs, better food in the schools, feeding the people in her community. And that's why they used to call her The Hell Lady of the Bronx. She had no problem with cursing a congressman, an assemblyman, a councilmember—because, in essence, they worked for her, they worked for the people who elected them. She died, literally died, for her community, for the Bronx. She founded a program called United Bronx Parents and, thirty years later, it's being run by my mother.

It was those demonstrations on Washington, D.C., demonstrations on City Hall, demonstrations at the Board of Education—those are my fondest memories of the '70s, growing up. We're sitting here at Hostos Community College, one of the first CUNY colleges for Hispanic people, and, after a few years, the city wanted to close it. We literally took over the college and ran the classes ourselves. Period. We took over Lincoln Hospital because they didn't have methadone programs for the rising heroin abuse in the '60s and '70s. They didn't have tuberculosis programs; it was running rampant in East Harlem at the time. And the Young Lords were part of my mother's inner circle—so one phone call and you could get five thousand people to demonstrate. You don't see that today. You don't see that camaraderie, that unity, with anything.

The Young Lords were a group of students who were tired of being treated as second-class citizens, our equivalent of the Black Panthers out west. Some of the youth had no direction at that time, and recruitment came from gang members; they used to speak to the gang members, like Afrika Bambaataa. They would say, "Take all that knowledge and hatred you have for each other and turn it into something good and positive for your people and your community." There were gang members who then became political activists.

Me, being a young, chubby, big Angela Davis-afro-wearing kid at the time, I used my camera to document my scenery, my community. That picture of the young girl at the *Fort Apache* demonstrations was just one of the many demonstrations I photographed. *Fort Apache* was a film done around 1981 or 1982 that depicted blacks and Latinos as drug pushers, whores, pimps, murderers. My grandmother was like, "Hell no. That's not going to happen." A couple of phone calls and, there we were, back to the streets, demonstrating. We were able to shut down the movie from filming a couple of times. We actually met with Paul Newman and a couple of the producers. They came to the office and me with my grandmother and said, "Miss Antonetty, we know who you are. Please don't do this! We know who you are." And she said, "Give twenty jobs to minorities." And they did. And when the movie was first released, there was a disclaimer at the beginning of the movie that read, "This movie does not portray Latinos and blacks of the Bronx accurately." And we did it. It was a victory.

The vibe of the South Bronx at the time was very colorful, animated, happy-go-lucky, do what you want. I used to tell people I was from the South Bronx and they were like, "Oh, abandoned buildings, gangsters," but on the contrary—it was family back then. Yes, there were gangs and drugs back then, but there are gangs and drugs everywhere in this country. We were just more out in the open. But it was a good time. There were family values back then. If Miss Smith who was the next-door neighbor gave you that look because you were doing something wrong, you stopped what you were doing. You respected your elders. Lots of family unity and strength. There was unity. If Miss Smith in the next building lost her job and needed groceries for the week, the whole building would chip in. Yes, the Bronx was burning at the time. You didn't know if your building was going to be there the next day, because if you lived in an old tenement, your building might be marked for arson. But it was part of the time. You just picked up and moved on.

Hip hop grabbed me. I was into disco at the time. I was going to Bonds, Studio 54, Gotham East, Gotham West, the Garage, the Loft, listening to Larry Levan, the whole Electric Circus, all those places. Hip hop grabbed me. I was kind of drafted, kidnapped so to speak; and it has been the blessing of my life, because hip hop is the way I live today. It's a culture.

I got started in the early '70s with photography. I went to Columbia University. I was in Agnes Russell, the private school. I went there from kindergarten through second or third grade, something like that. I was shown my report card back in '72. It said, "Joe is great in photography." It's one of the things I picked up there. I just loved it at an early age. I mean, we're talking 1972—I must have been ten years old, eleven years old. I got my first camera in '75, '76, something like that, when I was about fourteen. The camera was a hobby. But I'll let you in on a little secret. I was a chubby little kid growing up. I used it as a communication tool, and it was great because women—girls at that time—loved to be photographed. I was taking pictures throughout high school. In my junior year, I was the school photographer also. The yearbook photographer. Easy AD from the Cold Crush Brothers, DJ Tony Tone from the Cold Crush Brothers, and a few obscure MCs all went to my high school, South Bronx High School.

My first awareness of hip hop—the music—was being invited by Tony Tone to photograph a jam, a show of his. And that was at this little club that the Cold Crush used to perform at called Your Spot at Webster Avenue and 181st Street. There must have been about twenty people in this little club there. And I photographed them. It must have been '78, '79. I had known Tony for about a year prior to that. I had known AD before, because AD was a strong basketball player. But it wasn't until I started taking pictures of the basketball team during school that we got to know each other more. One of the reasons that I was invited to come was to take pictures of the formation of this group that they were trying to put together. I wasn't really liked by the group in the beginning because they had such a stature about themselves. I had to earn my respect from them.

One of the things that's difficult to realize is just how gigantic these shows were. There was such a following! From one year to another, it just blew up. I mean locally, in the communities and stuff. It spread from the streets of the Bronx into Manhattan like wildfire. You couldn't get into some of the places that these guys were performing in. My access to the Cold Crush Brothers was amazing. I gained their trust as their photographer, and again, the camera was my way of communicating with people. Whether it was during a jam session of hip hop or walking down the streets, I just loved it. I just documented my culture, my surroundings.

Joe Conzo

BORN IN THE BRONX

JDL

JDL, a.k.a. Jerry Dee Lewis

My ties to hip hop date back to 1973, when the first jam was ever given. It was at 1520 Sedgwick Avenue on the west side of the Bronx. It was DJ Kool Herc and Coke La Rock playing, and it was the most prolific jam in the history of hip hop. He had these really big speakers that had the bass in your stomach and you could hear every instrument clearly. The people that were there were the first b-boys and b-girls, it looked like everybody that was somebody was there. You had Eldorado Mike, the Original Clark Kent, the Nigga Twins, Sa-Sa, Bo-Bo, James Bond, Rossy, Trixie, Miss Ann, Sister Bu, Li'l Bit, Phase 2, The Nine Crew—all the hustlers, players, and everybody else that had heard about the jam.

The music was early breakbeats like "It's Just Begun," "Bongo Rock," "Apache," "The Mexican," "Get Ready" by Rare Earth, "Yellow Sunshine," "Listen to Me," "Get Into Something," "Voodoo," "Hijack," and the James Brown classic "Give It Up Or Turn It Loose." There were more records he spun, but the ones I named were the standouts—even to this day at b-boy conventions, these joints are played.

After that, I went home and could not stop talking about that jam and I couldn't wait to go to the next one. There wasn't no MCs at that time, but Herc used to say things on the mic like, "This is where you jam with the jammers, freak with the freakers, and boogie with the boogiers," and then he would let everybody know that they were listening to the Herculoid sound system. Then Coke La Rock would get on the mic and shout out all the b-boys and b-girls with this echo chamber that they had hooked up to the system, and it sounded so dope that you would hope that he would rock your name on it, because that would have meant that you was somebody. I would go home after each jam and recite some of what Herc said and put my name in it or my people's names. There weren't any rhymes being said at this time, but the first rhyme that was ever said was, "Dip dive and socialize and cut out all that bullshit jive / put your body in the park, your feet in check 'cause we are the kings of the discotheque / rock rock y'all." Now that rhyme went all around and each time somebody else said it they put their little twist on. By the time I said it, it went like this: "Ya dippy dippy dive ya so socialize ya clean out ya ears and ya open your eyes / and if ya can't do that then you must be wack so take two steps back and catch a heart attack / freak freak y'all to the beat y'all rock rock y'all and don't stop!"

I never wanted to be like everybody else, especially in rhyming, because I wanted to stand out and have my own identity. There was another DJ that no one hardly ever speaks about, but was very influential in the early origins of hip hop—his name is DJ Smokey, and he and his brother Rob the Gold, they were Kool Herc's archrivals. The differences between the two were that Kool Herc had the best sound system, but Smokey had more flavor, and he used sound effects and had breakbeats that Herc didn't have. The same people that went to Kool Herc parties also went to Smokey's, too! I can remember in my early b-boy days…that's right, I used to b-boy, too! As a matter of fact, everyone did before MC-ing and DJ-ing, except for Kool Herc—but he can bust a move if you force his hand. One time I was at a Smokey party at this spot called the Cage on 169th Street and Webster Avenue in the Bronx. I was there with my little crew, which consisted of me, Keith Bates, Barney Rubble, and Bombay, and I was dancing with this girl, miming this dance where I mix up a potion and drink it and turn into a mad scientist. Me doing this under a strobe light looks really ill, so when Keith Bates saw me breaking, he went ballistic and said, "Yo, you doing the Jerry Lewis—that's what I'm gonna start calling you, Jerry Lewis!" So everybody started calling me Jerry Lewis. At first I hated it, because it reminded me of the cartoon show and that stupid song, "Here come Jerry Lewis and he's right over there." I had to do something about the Jerry Lewis thing, so what I did was put the letter 'D' in between the Jerry and the Lewis and said it a couple of times…Jerry Dee Lewis Jerry Dee Lewis Jerry Dee Lewis…Yeah, that's it, because I thought if I was ever to get famous it had to be something that separated me from Jerry Lewis, a distinction so people would know which is which.

Now when MC-ing first came out, Keith Cowboy from Flash and the Furious Five MCs was the first one to rhyme, then Kid Creole, then Melle Mel. When I went to the Black Door and heard them with Flash on the turntables, it was crazy. I went home that night and said, "I can do that…" And I did! So I would go to the Flash parties, the Kool Herc parties, the Bambaataa parties, and go by the speaker and recite my rhymes to the beats that were playing regardless, whether an MC was on the mic rocking or not. In my head my rhymes were overriding the MC's rhymes, and sometimes mine sounded better.

One of my first rhymes was, "At the age of one I had a little fun, at the age of two I caught the boogaloo flu, at the age of three I was a death MC, at the age of four I had rhymes galore, at the age of five I made the crowd come alive, at the age of six I was king of the mix, at the age of seven my girl was eleven, and at the age of eight these rhymes I create, at the age of nine I was drinking wine, and at the age of ten I did it all again, so skip eleven and go to twelve, toot the horn and ring the bell. I rock 'em well y'all so swell y'all a Jerry Dee Jointski, over cups of coffee cause I don't drink tea y'all!" After that, I dubbed myself the rhymethologist and went from party to party looking for my shot to get on the mic and let it be known that I got skills!

It was 1977 when I first started rhyming on any microphone. But before that, I would test my rhymes out on the block I lived on, which was Burnside and University Avenue, on the west side of the Bronx. The kids that I hung out with were Butch Kid, Money Mooch, and Magic Fly. That was the crew of microphone gypsies I rolled with. I started rhyming long before them, but since we lived on the same block and hung out together, they started rhyming too. We would beat on cars all day rhyming. Then on the weekends I would go to whatever party was going on. It was still the era of the house party and no matter where the party was at, I was there. And if my boys did not go with me I would tell them how it was and what they missed out on. The reason they couldn't go was because most of them had curfews and had to be in by 10pm. Me too, but I didn't abide by the rules my mother gave me when it came to music. I love music just as much as life itself. It's something about music that soothes the soul and takes me anyplace I want to go. So I got a whole lot of whippings behind going to these parties and coming home all times of the morning. But was it worth it? Hands down without a shadow of a doubt. So it still wasn't no real MCs out there besides Keith Cowboy, the Kid Creole, Melle Mel, Grandmaster Casanova Fly, Lovebug Starski, and Busy Bee Starski. There wasn't no one that was rhyming on my side of town but me and my little crew. But out of my crew I was the only one that took it very seriously.

So now the summer of 1977 came and a lot of DJs had bought equipment and started bringing it outside and throwing jams in the schoolyard and on dead-end blocks. The first jam I went to and got on the mic was at 82 Schoolyard on Tremont and University Avenue. It was about two long blocks from my block so we walked up there and chilled in the background until the jam got packed and was almost rocking. About 9pm, me and my crew stepped under the ropes and I asked the DJ, "Can I get on the mic?" At first, he looked at me and my crew and recognized that we was from around the way, so he let me get on the microphone. I had whispered in my man Butch Kid's ear what records to get out of the crate to give to the DJ, who went by the name of DJ Whitehead, and his partner's name was Dr. Pepper. So Butch gave him "Let's Dance" by Pleasure, "I Can't Stop" by John Davis and the Monster Orchestra, "Catch a Groove" by Juice, "Seven Minutes of Funk" by the Whole Darn Family, "Funky Drummer" by James Brown, and the crowd-pleaser of all crowd-pleasers, "Take Me to the Mardi Gras" by Bob James (The Bells). So by the time Whitehead played The Bells, the party was rocking like crazy and I was throwing haymakers on the mic, freestyling people's names in the crowd I knew, doing a lot of different call-and-responses, and bigging up the DJ like hell. The feeling I had while rocking on the mic and watching the crowd respond to me at the same time was indescribable—and if I had to describe it in one word I would have to say orgasmic, to the tenth power. After I got off the mic, people came up to me and told me that I rocked it, that I was nice on the mic, and so forth and so on. I took it all in stride and went home and thought about the night and felt really good about myself, because tomorrow, people would be talking about what I did last night.

That summer was the best for me, because I established myself as an MC to be taken seriously and the west side was mine! The next year I was rocking even harder than the previous year and developed a real variety throughout the Bronx and in parts of Manhattan. My name, Jerry Dee Lewis, became "Jerry D," because the D was easy to rhyme. But one time at this party at Cisco's on Davidson Avenue and Burnside, we were all rocking it hard body, dusted up and what not, and Magic Fly got on the mic and started freestyling, and said this rhyme: "Jerry D Lewis or JDL, rockin' you well to the depths of hell." And the way he put the "JDL" in the rhyme sounded real fly, so fly that I started using JDL from then on as my name! So you can say that was the birth of JDL, I credit Magic Fly for that.

A couple of days later, DJ Whitehead came and asked if me and Butch Kid wanted to get down with him, and we said no. We didn't want to get down with nobody at the time. But we would like to go to his house and make a tape, and he said "Bet," so me and Butch went to his crib and made a dope tape. Me and Butch both had a copy. We listened to it over and over again on our block with the rest of our crew. I started going to more parties and jams on the east side of the Bronx, because they were more advanced than the DJs on the west side. The beats they were playing were crazy and I wanted to be rhyming on them joints, especially at Flash and Casanova Fly's parties,

because even though Herc's parties be packed, Flash and Casanova Fly's be rockin' hard! And all the girls be doing the new dance they called "the freak." So I would be at the Black Door, the Dixie Club, the Blue Lagoon, Webster PAL, Granny's, Walton Center, the Boys' Club that was around the corner from Roosevelt High School. In the winter, these spots was the place to be! Then you had the Bronx River Junior High School 123, Kips Bay Boys' Club, BAM, Disco King, Mario, Nicky D, Islam, and TryOne had that area on the smash. What I like the most about them joints was that you heard beats that you wasn't going to hear anywhere else, period. But you had to take that trip all up and across town to be in a part of the Bronx that if you really didn't know anybody you might get jumped. Did I care about any of that? No. Because a lot of people knew I could rhyme and used to see me all over, I knew a few people from all parts of the Bronx. Grandwizzard Theodore came out and Kevie Kev and his brother the Master Rob snatched Busy Bee up and started rhyming for Theodore and his two brothers, the amazing Mean Gene and the Incredible Coredio, and named themselves The L Brothers. Now I knew Kevie Kev and Rob from way back, since we used to play biddie basketball tournaments when we were young.

Being down with the crew really made me want to get down with a crew. But who? You just can't get down with a crew, a crew has to put you down with them. And you don't want to be down with any old crew, you want to be down with a crew that's got some juice—clientele. So I rhymed with Kool Herc for a minute, but I stopped because he didn't pay his MCs, because he told you that it was a privilege just to be rocking on the Herculoid sound system. I mean, it sounded good to them wannabe MCs, but not to me. So I bounced and kept doing my gypsy thing, going around from party to party, jam to jam, rocking the mic, building my clientele up. I was going to different DJs' houses, making tapes and selling them to cab services like OJ, Godfather, and Community Car Services to play for the young customers that wanted to hear hip hop.

The summertime came again and it was a whole lot of MCs and DJs that had cropped up over the winter, so there were going to be a lot of jams and parties for me to rock. This particular jam in 82 Schoolyard I'll never forget, because it was a turning point in my life. DJ Whitehead was rocking and for some strange reason it was crazy packed. I don't know, it could be karma, or kismet, but as I look at it now, it was the packest I've ever seen it. So anyway, I was in the back chilling, waiting for my time to get on the mic, which would be at about 9:30. So when the time came I went to the front of the ropes, went under, told Whitehead what to play and in what order, and then I cut the music off and made the crowd clap their hands to the beat. Then I counted it off and DJ Whitehead brought the music in, and from there on it was all me, the DJ, and the crowd, rocking and having a really good time. About six records into the set, Butch Kid came over to me and whispered into my ear that Casanova Fly just walked into the schoolyard, so I whispered back to him to give Whitehead some more joints to play. Butch gave Whitehead "Put the Music Where your Mouth is," "Breakthrough," "Scratchin," "Jonnie the Fox," "Congo," "Groove to Get Down," and "Apache." So now I'm rocking them hard with all my might, saying all my best rhymes, acknowledging DJ MC Grandmaster Casanova Fly being in the house—because the way he came in the schoolyard was like the coming of the king, with an entourage of two guys and about five girls with sweatshirts that had his name on them. And when I said that he was in the house he came to the front of the ropes and stood right in front of me while I was rocking. I wasn't nervous or anything—as a matter of fact, I didn't even look at him—I just kept on rocking the mic and moving the crowd. When I got off the mic, Casanova sent his partner, DJ Mighty Mike, over to talk to me, so while me and Butch were sharing a quart of Old English 800, DJ Mighty Mike told me that I was nice and that I had rocked it. I thanked him, he asked me if I knew who he was, and I said yeah. So then he asked me, did I want to rock with him and Casanova Fly at the Audubon Ballroom on October 6, and I said yes, on one condition—that

I start off as the head of the MCs. I knew that they had two MCs that were down with them, their names were the Prince Whipper Whip and MC Dottie Dot. Mike then explained to me that Whip was the head of the MCs, and I told him that I'm better than him and if need be, I'll battle him for the spot. And he said, "Bet. Come to Casanova's house tomorrow at 4pm."

The next day, me and Butch Kid went to Caz's house about half an hour early, and Whipper Whip and Dottie Dot were waiting outside for Caz also. So me and Butch said what's up and noticed that they had rhyme books in their hands, and we started laughing to ourselves because that was the first time we had seen anybody with a rhyme book. Caz came and we went inside, smoked some weed, and then went into the living room and Caz put a tape in the recorder, set some records up, and threw me the microphone to start the tape. I came there to battle straight up, but I didn't say anything. So I started the tape with the main introduction and hit Caz with an ill queue for him to come in, and then I just went ballistic. By the time Caz played the third record he'd seen that I wasn't no joke, cut the tape off, and said, "Yeah, you starting off the MCs at the Audubon." Whip and them all left and I stayed around and just vibed with Caz for hours, telling him all that I knew about him and how much I admired him and how much of an honor it was to be down with him. The Audubon show came, and it was the party of the year. All of the DJs that was on the flyer was there, and when our time came to get on, our system didn't work right, so we got on the L Brothers' sound system and rocked the house. Butch Kid had got down with DJ Whitehead and did the Disco DJ thing. We were still cool and will always be for the rest of our lives.

Being down with Casanova Fly was the ultimate, I mean there is no one smoother, no one flyer, no one that has more finesse, style, and grace than him. Still to this day, he is the epitome of what a DJ, MC, and living legend should be. So we started practicing every day as a group, The Mighty Force, and was building a name for ourselves with Caz being the focal point of the group, which was really cool because I was really learning a lot from him. He taught me how to mix, also—I already knew how to cut and scratch, but to mix is something different altogether, and Caz was the doctor of the mix. His style of DJ-ing was his to the point where if a DJ did something that he was known for, the crowd would let that DJ know right there on the spot, and that DJ would get booed off the stage. He had records that no other DJ had, and when he played them at a party, he rocked the crowd like crazy. He also had a special metal plate record that he got made at Angel's Sound in midtown Manhattan that was one-of-a-kind and made other DJs go out and get some made. What I like about him best was everything about him, and to this day, he's my very best friend in the whole wide world.

I remember when we played at The Sparkle, which used to be the executive playhouse on Mount Eden and Jerome Avenue in the Bronx. This bouncer that worked there named Hank dug us and wound up being our manager. This is the same person that Caz gave the rhymes to for "Rapper's Delight" (Big Bank Hank), and who didn't get a dime for it—but that's Caz's story, and trust me, when it's his turn he'll tell his story to the fullest! So after that fiasco with Big Bank Hank we was still rockin' and doing our thing but Whipper Whip and Dottie Dot, who changed his name to Dotta Rock, left us to get down with Grandwizzard Theodore, MCs Kevie Kev and Master Rob, and had formed The Fantastic Romantic Five MCs. We, on the other hand, had recruited two MCs (Little Gee and Lewie Lew) and changed our name to the Force Five, and were still doing shows. But most of all we were close-knit, meaning that we were hanging out all the time and growing up together. Little Gee went to the service and Lewie Lew went to jail, so me and Caz just stayed together and reinvented ourselves as the Notorious Two, and battled any and all duo MCs, taking them out crew by crew. One time me and Caz even took out a four-man MC crew—just me and him—matter of fact, it was the Imperial Brothers, 'cause I ain't scared to say their name! Yeah, me and Caz took them out in this club called Your Spot that used to be an old Burger King on Webster Avenue. We took out Jekyll and Hyde, Mr. Bond and Elmo,

Rave On and Johnny Wah, and a couple other duo MCs that were so wack I can't remember their names. So whenever there was a big show me and Caz was always on the card as the Notorious Two.

Another really great day in my life, as well as hip hop, was at the PAL on Webster Avenue, when they had an MC convention with all of the MCs from the five boroughs being in attendance. So me and Caz were in the back of the jam, with some girls, you know, doing what we do, and Charlie Chase and Tony Tone came back there to talk to Caz. They said what's up, and asked Caz if they could talk to him in private. Caz in turn said they can say what they had to say in front of me, because we were down together. They told Caz that they were starting a group called The Cold Crush Brothers, and they wanted Caz to be the head of the MCs, and that he could pick the other MCs at Charlie's house tomorrow, 'cause he was having auditions there. Caz said bet, under the condition that I was down also. Chase said no, because I was crazy and I be smoking angel dust and grabbing the mic from MCs with no respect for them—which was true. 'Cause if I'm at a party and the MC is not doing what he's supposed to be doing, I'm taking the mic from him or her and rocking down the house like it's supposed to be rocked. So then Caz said, "I'm down with JDL, and if he ain't down then I'm not down." So Chase said to Tone, "What do you think?" And Tone said, "The kid is nice, Chase, give him a shot." Chase said, "Come tomorrow and try out." I replied, "I don't try out for crews. I get put down with crews." And that was that! Me and Caz was down with Charlie Chase and Tony Tone, and hence the foundation of The Cold Crush Brothers was laid down!

The next day me and Caz rolled over to Chase's crib on 180th Street, by Junior High School 118, Notorious Two–style, rocking the same gear but different colors. When we got there Chase was on the turntables and the MCs were getting ready to get on the mic. This all-girl crew called Mercedes Ladies were there also chilling out, I think Chase went out with one of them. Chase and Tone had the system booming, mad loud, clear, and with crazy bass. Tone spoke to Caz and informed him this MC named Easy AD is automatically down 'cause they all went to school together [South Bronx High School]. So we talked to AD and he let us know that he used to be down with this crew called the Asalam Brothers, from around the Hoe Avenue area. So I was like, "What's that, like an all-Muslim crew?" And he was like, "Yeah!" I was laughing to myself thinking about an all-Muslim crew.

So the tryouts started, and it was a joke. When you're an MC, you analyze MCs differently from a fan, so just about all of them didn't have any skills except for two, this kid named Dynamite Tee and Kay Gee. Dynamite was half-assed, his problem was he "yes yes y'all-ed" through most of his rhyming. But Kay Gee had the voice that's in a class by itself, and he had a few rhymes that was all right, and to top it off he could freestyle. So Caz picked the dark-skinned kid named The Almighty KG. I had seen Kay Gee at jams rocking all over the Bronx and plus he was down with the Cheeba Crew from Webster Projects. And I liked him as a person, too, so I had no problems with rocking in the same crew as Kay Gee.

So now it's four MCs and two DJs and we had a party at South Bronx High School in two weeks, so Caz told us that we would be practicing at his house every day from 4pm to 8pm (Sundays too!). The next day at Caz's house we went through some names for us and settled on the Cold Crush Four. So now it's the Cold Crush Brothers featuring the Cold Crush Four. We started brainstorming for some harmonies to do and the first one was off the "We Will Rock You" song by Queen, followed up with "Stiletto" from Billy Joel's 52nd Street album. The next one was called "I'm Testing," so we got those down pat for the South Bronx party, and when that party came, it was packed wall to wall. So what we did was let Chase start the party off playing the newest joints that had just come out. Then we got on one by one, and at the height of the party all four of us got on and hit 'em with mad crowd participation stuff, then spanked 'em with our two new routines, and rocked them.

When we was on I noticed this Puerto Rican kid taking pictures of us from all angles, like he was down with a magazine or something. Later on that night Chase introduced him to us and told us that he went to South Bronx also with Tony Tone and Easy AD. His name was Joey Kane, and he had the mad big afro and was cool as hell, too! Another dude who had plugged in a cassette recorder into the mixer and made tapes went to school with them, too. His name was Sammy but he was called Tapemaster. Plus, Tone's two brothers, King and KK, Chase's record passer Flashski, and some guys who used to help carry the equipment and double as security—Big Al (Italian Stallion), Jerry, and Herk. So all these guys plus us are the Cold Crush Brothers, and when we rolled, we rolled deep! After that night at South Bronx High School, practice resumed at Caz's house every day. We decided we wasn't doing any parties for a while because groups were doing their thing, and had a few routines, and was getting mad juice—so we had to come correct our next time out. You had the Furious Five, the Funky 4 Plus 1, the Fantastic Romantic Five, the Treacherous Three, Crash Crew, Soul Sonic Force, Cosmic Force, Jazzy Five, Fearless Four, Death Committee... and they all had routines and harmonies. However, most of them had stuff from TV shows or commercials, like F Troop, Gilligan's Island, Crazy Eddie, Jordache, Oscar Meyer—you know, cartoon kiddie stuff, and we didn't want to fall in that same paradox. So we had to come up with something different, something new, and something that would make us stand out from the rest.

So Caz, me, AD, and Kay Gee brainstormed, pooled our thoughts and pros and cons, all our ideals—then Kay Gee came out of the blue and said, "Caz, let's do a joint off of that white boy record 'Cat's in the Cradle,'" and hummed the melody with this breakbeat by Gerrone called "Rock It in the Pocket." And it was crazy, you hear me? Crazy dope, fresh, the joint and every other hip slang that was out then (word!). So Caz put the lyrics to it and said, "Yeah, it's hittin', but we need at least one more to come behind it." And here go Kay Gee again with the "Alone Again Naturally" joint off the same breakbeat! I stayed after practice with Caz to put the finishing touches on the two dope routines that would let everybody know in hip hop that Cold Crush will be a force to be reckoned with! We rehearsed the two joints for three weeks, hard, over and over and over again, 'til we had it down pat to a tee, then made up "It's Us" and "Isn't He the Sureshot" off of "Love Rap." That and mad freestyle stuff we already had, made us sound tight and different from the other groups.

Now we were ready to put it to the test. Well, that night came at this show they had at this club called C&C Disco on 125th Street and Lenox Avenue in Harlem (over the Lenox Lounge). Crash Crew, Fantastic Five, and us the Cold Crush Four was playing there that night. So first Crash Crew got on and did their little thing, then Fantastic got the party in full swing with Grandwizzard Theodore cutting like crazy. Then it was our turn. In the dressing room Caz ran down the order of the routines, and when we got on the stage and tested the mics, I don't know about the rest of the crew, but I had this semi-nervous feeling in my stomach—just like I got now as I'm writing this, 'cause I'm going through the emotions like it's all happening now. So we test the mics and right before we start I smiled at Caz, and it wasn't a regular smile, it was a smile that said, "We are going to rip this stage." And that's just what we did! Ripped it! And that's my word on everything that I love! Everybody that was there, even the groups that performed were in awe because they had never seen it like that or heard it that fly. But the one thing that really messed their heads up was that we kept it real humble when we got off stage, and when people told us that we rocked it, we said, "We try, man, we try." We also knew that we couldn't stop there or get complacent, so we went back into the batcave the next day and topped what we had in our arsenal by busting out with two more routines off of Love Rap.

A year went by, and in that time we went from local to eastern seaboard and then some! Always making sure we practiced, staying humble, and most of all staying hungry. The thing I want to touch on right now is the love we had for each other, and, more importantly, love for the art form. We always hung out together whether practicing or just giving out flyers, snapping on each other and stuff. The best times of my life were with the Cold Crush Brothers. I don't think there are a better set of guys than them. The reason I say this is because I been on my own since the age of sixteen, when I started rhyming, and it's been rough. When I hooked up with Caz and then the Cold Crush they took me in without a second thought and showed me unconditional love, the kind I really didn't get from my family—but then again I did, because the Cold Crush Brothers is my family! We took all the talent we had, pushed ourselves to the limit, always thought out of the box and created a name for ourselves that will never, ever be forgotten. When you look through the history of hip hop from the beginning you will see as well as read about the Cold Crush Brothers. If I had to say what made us what we are today—legendary—I would have to say our presence, our showmanship, our trendsetting ways, and most notably our battle skills. From 1981 to 1983, every boom box, every OJ, Godfather, Touch of Class car service, was playing nothing but Cold Crush tapes from every place we played. In Brooklyn, cats stuck dudes up for Cold Crush tapes. In Queens, cats were paying twenty dollars for Cold Crush tapes. I mean, we were on top of our game like no one else! Numerous best stage show awards, never lost in a MC convention, and battles', we only lost one out of maybe a hundred. And if you listen to the tape of the battle we lost—Cold Crush vs. Fantastic Five—we were robbed of that one!

Matter of fact, that night of July 3rd 1981 in Harlem World, when we battled the Fantastic Five, was both a gift and a curse for us. The curse was that we didn't get on last that night, and one thing I learned in life is that people only remember what they last saw or heard! But that night when we came out with the gangster suits, the gangster brims and machine guns, was a gift. It was a gift because we learned a valuable lesson in that loss, and used that as strength to hone our craft to the point that we would never go through a night like that again, and we never did, never! The only alliances we kept after that were the Treacherous Three, Fearless Four, and Dougie Fresh. Everybody else got the business of being crushed to the fullest extent of our law. Our stage show was to the tenth power from what everybody else was doing. We were using smoke machines, powder blasts, throwing eight-by-ten-inch glossy pictures and posters of us in the crowd, and one time when we won one of them MC contests, Caz threw the prize money into the crowd, caused a pandemonium riot while we left the building! The thing about us was that we had so many routines, so many dance steps and mad stage entrances, that when we performed, you didn't know what we were going to do or how we were coming out on stage. All you knew for sure was that the Cold Crush was getting ready to perform and you can't miss it.

That's what I love about Joey Kane and his impeccable photography skills. He didn't miss a show or an event, so he has the proof to what I'm saying. All through our reign, Joey took pictures, Tapemaster recorded the shows, Tony Tone made sure our Cold Crush system had the bass in your face, Charlie Chase was cutting it up straight, no chaser, and the cold crushing motherfucking tough-ass four MCs blew your goddam mind! The first MCs ever to take classic rock songs and flip them into hip hop routines. The first MCs to use stage props! The first MCs to go to Japan, and we were in the first hip hop movie, Wildstyle. And you want to hear something funny? We never made an album, just a few singles. Records were never our forte: we dominated where it counted. That stage, that's our claim to fame, and will go down in history as such! I have no regrets about being a part of the iconic, the world renowned, the legendary Cold Crush Brothers, featuring the cold crushing motherfucking tough-ass four MCs!

JDL a.k.a. JERRY D LEWIS
The man, the myth, the legend, the untold truth!
Cold Crush 4 Life

CASANOVA FLY

GRANDMASTER CAZ

April 18th, 1960, Curtis Brown was born in the Bronx, New York City. Thirteen years later, a culture was born just blocks away from his family's four-room apartment. The culture is called hip hop and the witness to it, Curtis Brown, is me—Grandmaster Caz. I not only witnessed the birth of hip hop but the elements which make up its foundations. Being a child of the '60s and '70s I grew up in the Bronx when the worst things you could say about the Bronx were true. Abandoned buildings and burnt-down tenements, slumlords and vacant lots strewn with garbage and burnt remains. The greatest city in the world was bankrupt and corrupt. But from these conditions arose a culture that would eventually take the world by storm. Hip hop for some is just the music they hear on the radio followed by the accompanying video. That's the marketing and selling of one of the elements of hip hop culture. But hip hop as a whole is so much more.

Back in the day (mid- to late-1970s), hip hop was free and it was live. True hip hop has to be witnessed and participated in. In the Bronx's early hip hop days, there was a process involved in hip hop that was before the party even happened. It was the preparation, shopping for records that nobody had yet or that perfect break, the sound system that, as a DJ, you had to have. Practicing your b-boy moves before the jam so you could be ready for whoever might try to step up to the plate. Your gear was another thing. There were always a lot of girls at the jams so you had to be fresh. Securing transportation for equipment and crew and the whole nine was a trip, and for what? Just to keep our party alive. You see at thirteen, fourteen, fifteen, none of us could get into discos. You had to wear shoes and slacks and collared shirts. Who wants to get dressed up to spin around on the floor? We had our own style, our own music, and our own crowd.

Hip hop saved the Bronx from what could've been Little Rock, Arkansas in the nineties. The birth of hip hop coincided with the end of the gang movement in New York. Prior to hip hop, the most popular pastimes were sports, music, drugs, and gangs. Not a lot of high profile pimps in the Bronx, or I might have chosen a different vocation. However, hip hop seemed to convert even the most negative and violent intentions into healthy and competitive ones. Gangs turned into crews and organizations. Battles took place in b-boy circles instead of empty lots. The weapons of choice were now moves and talk of prowess and bravado. Strength was shown in power of sound, instead of numbers. It was a great time to grow up in the Bronx. To witness the transition of a society and play a role in it is one of the most fulfilling things I have been blessed to be a part of.

As a young b-boy I took the name Casanova Fly because the rest of the crew had Casanova names. Black, Mack, Red—so I chose Fly. There's probably a photo somewhere in this book so you can see why. Before that, me and my boy Troy used to practice breaking in my house. I jacked some old soul and R&B joints from my big sister and started my record collection. I found some of my first breaks on those albums. *Soul Makoosa* by Manu DiBango. The Fatback Band's *Street Music*, and of course the Godfather of Soul, James Brown's *Hell* album and the live *Sex Machine* album with the classic "Give It Up Or Turn It Loose" break. This was when I was living up the block from DJ Kool Herc. It was his sister's party at 1520 Sedgwick Avenue that changed the way we partied forever. From there, the race was on for hip hop supremacy. Every neighborhood in the Bronx had its local DJ or crew of DJs. Uptown Bronx was DJ Breakout and Baron of the Brothers Disco and

Grandmixer DST. The East had Kool DJ D and Tyrone, Disco King Mario, Afrika Islam and of course Afrika Bambaataa, Jazzy Jay, and the mighty Zulu Nation in Bronx River. South Bronx was Grandmaster Flash, the L Brothers, Love Bug Starski, and Kool DJ AJ. There were a lot of local cats who never graduated beyond "Hip Hop High" but were early participants in the culture. The Bronx was soon flooded with eager participants and hip hop hopefuls. Crowds would walk fifteen to twenty-five blocks to get to an outside jam. All you had to do was ask, "where they jammin'?" and follow the crowd until you hear the music.

When hip hop had to go inside, a host of Bronx clubs took our music and our followers in and allowed us to continue our party, our way. The Hevelo, the Sparkle, the Dixie Club, the Ecstasy Garage, the T-Connection, the Black Door, the Blue Lagoon and many more, all located in the Bronx. The hundreds of parks, school yards, side streets, gymnasiums, community centers, ballrooms and catering halls have all been instrumental in providing a place for us to keep hip hop alive. The City of New York for unknowingly providing the electricity through the many street light poles from which we powered our amps, mixers and turntables for outdoor jams also deserves some credit. Even New York's finest get love for not being the assholes they could've been on numerous occasions. Eight times out of ten they would walk or drive past our jams and not stop or pull our plug. They seemed to realize that we had found something creative to do, and figured, "well at least we know where everybody is!" In the days and months that followed its inception, word slowly leaked about this new style of art, dancing, DJ-ing, and talking on the microphone over beats. First Harlem, and then Queens, Brooklyn, Staten Island, Long Island, the tri-state area, the country, and eventually the world. But it all started in my hometown, my borough, my hood. That's right y'all—me and hip hop, born in the Bronx!

Grandmaster Caz
2007

Johan Kugelberg: So when these records originally came out, you guys dismissed them completely.

Grandmaster Caz: No doubt. See, the early and the first crop of rappers and DJs and MC pioneers, true pioneers, anything that wasn't on par, up to standard, so to speak, with the standards that we had set, we dismissed. There were a lot of crews that were around while we were around, but we didn't give them the time of day because they weren't as good as we were. So we kind of dismissed them. So when the record thing came along, the same thing happened. These guys had come out from an obscure place, we had never heard of them, no one had ever heard of them, and they're making attempts at doing what we do as a craft. So we pretty much dismissed it. But it is all valid. Looking back on it now, some of them are pretty good!

JK: Yeah, you heard a lot of these records for the first time as we were working on this project.

GMC: Exactly. Working on this project, some of these records I never heard of. And like I said, these were records we dismissed just looking at them.

I mean, even as a DJ, you give me a record called "Rollerskate Rap," I'm not playing that. I'm not even going to listen to it. And a lot of this stuff just got dismissed. If it didn't stick to the wall, it really didn't show up on the radar. Everybody can't be at the beginning. So I'm not asking, "Where were you in '74?" But when you talk about old-school and pioneers and making a mark and being in that class of people who laid that groundwork that everybody followed from, that's an era before 1978 and 1979—even up to 1977, when MC-ing started becoming more of an art than people just saying random stuff on the mic.

JK: So even the first time people extended the break on "Let There be Drums" or "Funky Drummer" or something like that, when were you guys aware of that?

GMC: In 1975, 1976. I remember the advent of 12-inches.

JK: Yeah, 1976.

GMC: There were no 12-inches before that. Disco brought in the era of the 12-inch 45s, so that was where we looked for new breaks. That was an explosion in '76, all year and every week, a flood of new records hit. And to be a DJ, you've got to keep up with everything. So at one point, we're buying everything that comes, because there isn't anything else. This is the start of this. I remember the first disco record, the first 12-inch 45. First we'll buy that and on up until you get there. So that was the main source for looking for breaks after that. Before that, it was older records, looking in for old James Brown and stuff like that.

JK: The R&B records.

GMC: Yeah. That was a new source of breaks and a different place to dig.

JK: Was there an awareness of the Jamaican tradition, of toasting, of the sound system?

GMC: Not really. We never really realized that that was Kool Herc's background, and that's where the large sound system came from, and that the DJ was the MC over there and the MC was the DJ. It is an opposite but it's the same thing that we do. But we had no idea 'til later on, until reggae started to play a bigger role in popular music.

JK: Which of the original fellas had Jamaican heritage? I know Herc, and Flash is from the Caribbean, no? Any of the other ones?

GMC: Flash was born in the Bronx but I think his heritage is Bahamas. But you know, it's not like they're walking around eating cow peas and stuff in the house. They New York! And I find that a lot of the early and today's hip hop artists who really kind of shine through have that Jamaican or Caribbean heritage—Doug E Fresh and a lot of cats like that. I'm like, wow. I mean, I was adopted so I don't really know, but I could have a Jamaican bloodline myself.

JK: I can see, as far as the lust for life and the larger-than-life persona, that there might be some Jamaican flow hiding back a couple of generations.

GMC: But we didn't really realize the heritage and the culture of the Jamaican thing, the DJ thing—this was new for us. I remember block parties when I was a little kid, when they used to—not every week, not like a jam like we used to do it—but they would play music and have all the little kids out there dancing, and they'd make a big circle, and the best dancing kids, they'd shoo 'em into the middle of the circle. And I remember being little, doing James Brown moves and stuff like that. So the block party was nothing new. But this is a reinvention of something, that that energy came about again and we needed to get out there.

JK: It's a New York block party, and into that New York block party was brought the power of the Jamaican sound system.

GMC: Exactly. Hip hop brought that. Prior to that, it didn't matter you got little speakers, as long as you could hear music out there. There wasn't the thing of having this large sound system. Herc brought that to the table—he set the standard.

JK: In your opinion, who were the first to follow Herc's leads, as far as other competing sound systems go?

Grandmaster Caz, a.k.a. Casanova Fly

GMC: Breakout and Baron—the mighty Sasquatch sound system—they had pretty much homemade stuff, but their stuff was big, powerful.

JK: Yeah, it was fantastic.

GMC: Flash, it couldn't rival Herc's system at no point. Me, I couldn't compete. My sound system couldn't even compete with none of that.

JK: We are still talking pre-blackout.

GMC: Yeah, we talking pre-blackout, so Herc pretty much set the standard.

JK: But one important statement to be made is that the New York City blackout of 1977, maybe it didn't give birth to hip hop, but it certainly was responsible for the newborn getting really quality formula to drink, if you know what I'm saying.

GMC: Most definitely. I was lucky to have the money to buy my sound system early on, and I had the bottom of the barrel, like the starter kit, the hip hop starter kit, so to speak. So to have the amount of equipment on the level that Herc had, you needed money. And not a lot of us had that, so when the blackout happened in '77, I mean, they broke in everything in the city, especially the electronics stores. Because they knew. "We can sell turntables—the DJs is hip, people want to be DJs and stuff." And so many DJs popped up the next day and week after that blackout, it was ridiculous. People were playing music, you'd see little, young DJs smokin' on little blocks, you know? It was just crazy.

JK: What about activity in other boroughs? What about the disco DJs that sort of had their feelers in the world of hip hop?

GMC: That's also something that a lot of us overlooked, being we are from one place. I'm from the Bronx. I've got people who live in Queens, but basically I'm from the Bronx. Everything I'm trying to do is right here in the Bronx. So we are not looking at what's happening in Brooklyn. No one was making that kind of noise in another borough, as far as hip hop was concerned, for us to think that it was going on somewhere else.

JK: Was there awareness of the people that were, like, older DJs and radio DJs?

GMC: Most definitely. Everybody's early influence. Herc brought hip hop to the street, brought that disco and DJ-ing element to the street. So we were aware of the Hollywoods, like the Flowers, Hollywood, Eddie Cheeba, Pete DJ Jones, the guys like that who played in the clubs. But we couldn't get into clubs—we were kids.

JK: As far as just the idea of breakbeats and break DJs, who do you see as the true pioneers of that?

GMC: Kool Herc.

JK: And as far as just extending those breaks longer and longer?

GMC: I'd have to give that to Flash. Herc would have two of the same record but he would bring 'em in indiscriminately. It's not like he was on time, like, when this beat was "boom," he'd get right in. He'd just let it go. Flash synchronized it.

JK: And Herc, in that glorious Jamaican tradition, washed off the labels. Scratched off the labels.

GMC: He was the master of that. He let us know, "I ain't letting y'all see what this record is. You gotta find it for yourself." That's the whole thing about the records that I got—so why would I tell all the other DJs what my records are?

JK: Did you guys go into the city to buy records?

GMC: Yeah. We had more sources of records because record stores were all over the place, back in the day. Right now, they don't sell records anymore. But there was a store called Crazy Eddie's, electronics chains and big record shops. That was the main place, they had bins and bins of records there. And then a few specialty shops would open up where we knew people who worked there, and they gave us a lead on, "This is where the breaks are, the joints that y'all look for." So we started going there, like Downstairs Records, which was in the train station down downtown.

JK: How would you describe the growth curve of when it started getting into the clubs—the first time hip hop really started coming off the streets? What do you remember as the very first?

GMC: I would say 1977. I mean, it was in the clubs since early. Herc was in the club. But when hip hop started in clubs, period, I would say '77, '78. You could go to a general club and some hip hop would be going on. Plus, we had to find a place to keep hip hop going on over the winter. Hip hop started in the summertime and then we took it out to the parks. Once the little rooms became too small, we had to go somewhere where everybody could fit in the party. There's no better place than outdoors. So that's why the parks and the schoolyards. When it started getting cold in the wintertime, where we gonna go? We can't play hip hop now, it's snowing or it's raining. So what are you saying to us, "No hip hop 'til next summer?" Hell, no. We gotta go to these clubs and some of these venues and ask them, "Can we have hip hop?" I was fourteen, fifteen years old going to clubs, nightclubs, like, "My name is DJ Casanova Fly. I have a following of people who come to my parties and I want a night in your club. We charge this amount, we'll split the door. You take half and we take half."

JK: Why do you think that there was such a gigantic time delay before hip hop went onto wax?

GMC: I think because it hadn't spread wide enough for people to think that it would catch on. It was like something that kids do.

JK: But the tapes sold in large quantities.

GMC: They sold locally, though.

JK: How many copies of the tape would you be able to sell if it was a hot tape? Five hundred?

GMC: Not even. We wasn't even on that number. Over the years, I've sold thousands of tapes. I'm platinum. But it was whoever was the fan of hip hop, the people who used to come to the jams. Everybody didn't have access to this music. We as DJs, we went out and we sought out the music. It wasn't like it was mix tapes out here with everything. If you wanted to hear them beats in them songs and you didn't have them at home, or your ma didn't have them, you had to come to our party to hear them. Until the disco records came out, stuff like that, which everybody had, everybody could go get. That was pop music, that was popular music of that day, so you could just go buy that record if you wanted. But the beats and the joints that they didn't know what it was, people didn't know the names of, they might have had it right at home in their records but they didn't know what it was. They had to come to the jam to hear. And if not, you had to buy a tape. And later on, people started selling the records.

JK: Breakbeat Lenny selling copies of every deleted 45 with a drum break

on it. As far as that strange transition from a performed culture to a recording culture goes, when did you guys become aware of record companies? When did Mr. Robinson of Enjoy Records and Mrs. Robinson of Sugarhill Records show up?

GMC: In 1978, 1979, pretty much. We were aware that the possibility of this being put on a record was a little more real. Before, we never even thought about it. And we were more at the performance level.

JK: You were selling huge tickets; you were drawing really big crowds.

GMC: Yeah, we had a fire. Everywhere we go, our shit was packed. We was headlining. We were doing shows with New Edition when they came out. We was headlining.

JK: How large were the crowds in '78, '79, before there were records, at the biggest?

GMC: Like, fifteen hundred, two thousand people. Depends on how big the venue was. On a regular basis, you get about four or five hundred people. You have to remember that we were live. We were more alive, we were more stage-orientated and performance. We weren't thinking about recording.

JK: You guys didn't really care.

GMC: We didn't care, especially from our group, the Cold Crush. It was, like, yeah, it was cool, it would be cool, but no, we really can't afford that, that tooth and nail. Y'all go ahead and do that, and if the right situation come along where we can do what we need to do, yeah, okay, cool. We got to a point where we felt we had to make a record. Okay, now it's getting to the point where you've got to have a record.

JK: But then we're already in 1980, 1981. So, in the beginning being on a record was considered somewhat abstract, that was something for mainstream artists only.

GMC: Right. So in '79, '80, when we did "Weekend," it was like, yo guys, do this. Somebody close to us, we didn't feel detached like we were signing to some company or nothin'. We did a record but we didn't really strive for that recording artist glory. Most of the guys came up. Most of them, from the Funky Four to the Furious Five to the Jazzy Five, to the Treacherous Three to the Soul Sonic Force, the Cosmic Force, all the Bambaataa crews, everybody came out with records. Everybody came out eventually. Spoonie Gee, the Manhattan crews, and I really can't think of any cats from the Bronx. Busy took a while before he came out with a record.

JK: Yeah, "School Groove," that's not until 1981.

GMC: Yeah, and you would have thought Busy would be at the forefront of that because he was one of the main solo MCs.

JK: But there weren't really labels seeking the music out, either.

GMC: No, not at all.

JK: You had Enjoy, you had Sugar Hill. And Robinson's brother had Holiday Records.

GMC: But we had no idea any of that stuff would stick to the wall, how serious it was. Because, like I said, majors made it painfully obvious that they wanted nothing to do with it.

JK: With the exception of Kurtis Blow.

GMC: Right, after Kurtis got signed. But then Kurtis was one of them disco rappers, that's how the rest of us are looking at it. Yeah, they'll sign that. "Don't you give me all that jive about things you wrote before I," we don't rhyme like that. You know what I mean.

JK: And of course, Kurtis Blow is comprehensive from a major record label standpoint, because he is the same kind of guy that the guys want to hear on the radio. Like DJ Hollywood, Eddie Cheba. That's an older crowd. The DJ crowd is an older crowd.

GMC: And they're looking at a buyer's market. Nowadays the buyer's market is younger. The hip hop market, they spend more money on all that stuff than anybody. But back then, the record company would have to take a chance, would say, okay, this is an older market here that we could capture messing with Kurtis Blow, as opposed to messing with them street rappers.

WE DESTROYED THAT PLACE

LA Sunshine

LA Sunshine

Unbeknownst to a lot of so-called hip hop historians, the original Treacherous Three members were LA Sunshine, Kool Moe Dee, and Spoonie G. Special K joined the group upon Spoonie's departure, which was brought about by Spoonie deciding to do a record without the group. K added a more rugged feel to the group with his Bronx style. Moe was always a technician and I had the most energy and "flava." We fed off of each other really well. It got to a point where we locked in so tight, there were times when people thought that there was only one of us rhyming, when in fact it would be all three of us splitting up a sentence. I honestly still have not seen that particular style perfected to that level since then. We took advantage of our vocal synchronicity by doing a lot of harmonizing. To quote a classic:

Because K is for Kool and S is for Sunshine and Special K
Because we're right on time
With originality in all our rhymes
Because to bite a rhyme is an MC crime
We'll rock the house, without a doubt
Young ladies said we're guaranteed to turn it out
And if you don't believe it's true
Just check out how we rock for you (so get funky).

As for writing rhymes—I never did. Do not get it twisted: I am in no way saying that I did not create my own lyrics, I just did not write them down. When we were in the studio recording a particular single, I would be putting my solo rhyme together in my head. Freestyle rhymes, those unrelated to a recorded song or a routine—at least that is what it meant back then—I would put together over a period of time. I would come up with an idea for a rhyme and just add to it every now and then. But I would do it all in my head and by the time it was finished I would have it memorized. For the most part, that is how my joints were formulated.

It is always a plus for any group when each member brings high-quality talent and creative input to the table. That was the case with the T-3. Moe came up with a lot of the concepts, K the harmonies, and I was a show perfectionist, so I was able to focus a lot on the dances. I can remember venturing out of the tri-state area for the first time, what an experience that was! We went on a tour of the south with dates in Greensboro, Raleigh, and Macon to name a few. Being on a bill with the likes of the Bar-kays, Cameo, and other bands—naturally, the audience was expecting to see instruments and not turntables ("Ya'll ain't no band, where is the bass player?"). We were heckled initially. But winning them over never was a problem, and by the time "[Feel the] Heartbeat" came on, we would have them in the palms of our hands.

We were eventually dropped from the tour because we became a problem for the bands. They did not expect us to be as sharp as we were, and we started getting more of a response than the headliners. We learned quickly that the griminess of the business did not end with the record labels. I was seventeen when we signed with Enjoy Records. We knew that the business was somewhat shady, but we could never have prepared for what was in store. Here we were, coming out with records that were doing well, touring with the hottest acts and beginning to make an impact on the industry in a way we did not in the streets and in the clubs. Then reality slapped me in the face when we received our first royalty payment. It came literally in a brown paper bag and was about one thousand dollars (to split). Now I know I was young, but stupid I was not, nor have I ever been.

That was the first time I started to doubt the business was for me. But, when we would come up with things like,

Rock the body body
Rock the body body
Rock the body body
Rock the body body

which Moe came up with while taking a—let's just say relieving himself… There was so much passion put into it that the love of the art would win out over the turmoil, and when we would perform in front of fans that were as passionate as we were, it made me stick with it.

I can remember one show in particular. It was billed as the show of all shows and was held at the Amory in Harlem. Initially we weren't on the card because the artists were all on Sugarhill Records—the likes of the Sugarhill Gang, Crash Crew, Sequence, Funky 4 plus 1, and of course the Furious Five, who we were in heavy competition with for the number one spot on the streets. But "[Feel the] Heartbeat" was so hot that we had to be added. Now being the only group not on their label, you know they tried to give us the business—smallest dressing room, no food or drinks in it, and it seemed like it was a mile away from the stage.

There has always been a high competition level in hip hop, but we knew that we would really have to bring our A-game that night. I think that one of our main attributes as a group is that we were always able to critique other groups objectively. Now most MCs or groups would never say that someone else was better on a particular night, not to mention a career. But I can truly say with the utmost certainty that we destroyed that place.

LA Sunshine
2007

SCRATCH CREATOR

Grandwizzard Theodore

I was born into a culture that changed my life and changed the world. My family loves music, my mother played a lot of music in the house. She played everything—James Brown, Earth Wind & Fire, Al Green, all Motown records, the blues, disco music. Now my brothers play a lot of music, like Dennis Coffey, Baby Huey, Kool and the Gang, Average White Band, Stevie Wonder… I could go on for days, but what I am trying to say is that the culture was growing as I grew.

Now as for us people in the streets, I saw graffiti on the trains, on the building walls, on peoples' shirts, on peoples' walls, in their houses, not knowing I was being exposed to a growing culture. And the way people talked with slang—and sometimes slang would change as time went by—this was part of the culture I was exposed to at the age of eight, when I finally started to notice all of this around me.

Now I loved to dance, ever since I can remember—dancing to James Brown for my family ever since I can remember. As I got older my love for the culture got stronger. I got exposed to DJ-ing through my brother, DJ Mean Gene, and Grandmaster Flash. I was a b-boy first because that was a way for me to show my stuff and express myself, but I loved DJ-ing so much I was willing to learn, not knowing I had a gift. But it was up to me to take it to the next level.

At the age of eleven I used to play my mother's 45s on her record player, and when the record got to the break I used to skip the record back. As time went by I started skipping the 45s like a loop, not knowing I was onto something. And as time went by my brother Mean Gene and Grandmaster Flash grew apart—Flash formed his own group and my brother and myself formed a group, the L Brothers, because my brother knew I had skills. No one sat me down to teach me how to DJ—my skills was ready, willing, and able. At the age of twelve I was unstoppable. Most of the DJs back then had trouble mixing two records, some DJs just stopped altogether. When I created the scratch nobody could understand what was happening, nobody could do it. I was the only DJ scratching until Flash finally got it, and then he created the back spin.

Some people claim that they created the scratch—but I know better. They were the DJs that retired after I created the scratch when I was in High School—Morris High School at 166th Street and Boston Road. My principal played music in the lunch room and people got tired of it. I had a guy I hung out with, he was outspoken, and he asked me to make a tape and gave it to the principal to take a listen. And when I made this tape I had to put the boombox up against the speaker and hope it sounded clear. Now the music was loud in my mom's house and she did not play games. When I was making this tape I created the scratch—you know the story and the rest is history.

We had two MCs, Kevie Kev and Robbie Rob. As time went by I decided to form my own group: Kev, Rob, Double Dee, and Busy Bee Starski. Busy Bee became a solo artist and we met Dottarock and Prince Whipper Whip and the Fantastic Five was formed, and the rest is history, filming the first hip hop movie *Wildstyle*, winning numerous MC battles…

As for myself, as time went by, my skills got better and no one ever questioned the fact that there is only one person who created the creation and the DJ skills I bring to this hip hop culture. As soon as the world gave me my props, that's when people started to come forward claiming to have created my creation. The scratch is something the hip hop culture cannot live without. I put a lot of hard work into this culture and nobody is going to take nothing from me. That's why I am still doing my thing and they are not. Thanks to Kool Herc, Bambaataa, Mean Gene, Flash, Rock Steady Crew, Tat's Cru, and all the graffiti writers around the New York City area. A lot of people died for this culture and aren't here anymore, like Keith Cowboy, Darryl C., BO, Wiz Kid, and so on—there are so many more names, you know who they are. I carry all those people with me when I perform. I've traveled around the world more times than I can remember, and this culture changed the world. This is the only culture that brought all the different cultures together as one—with that said, I continue to travel the world and teach people about hip hop.

Grandwizzard Theodore,
photo © Charlie Ahearn

God bless James Brown—without him there would be no hip hop. All people should look up the word "pioneer" so they would stop calling themselves pioneers. Some people get into the culture for the wrong reason, that's why their careers don't last that long. With that said: Long live hip hop!

Grandwizzard Theodore
Creator of the needledrop and the scratch
Date of birth: March 5, 1963
Birth of scratch: June, 1975
Date hip hop will end: Never

BUDDY ESQUIRE

Johan Kugelberg: When did you start to do artwork?

Buddy Esquire: I started doing that around the time I was writing graffiti. That was many moons ago; that started roughly 1972. And we really didn't get the trains until 1973.

JK: When did you make your first flyer?

BE: I knew Tony Tone back when I was going to Stevenson High School. My graffiti start was after I quit. I just kept going at it with the pen, you know, scratched it on paper, and I got better. And he was liking my style.

JK: Do you remember what the very first flyer was?

BE: Yes, I remember it very well. It was made in November of '78 for I.S. 131. I don't have a copy of that one right now, I wish I did. Actually, that's my second flyer. The first flyer I made for some outside jam back in '77.

JK: When did it start getting really frantic—just as far as the workload and how many flyers were churned out?

BE: After I started getting into design, instead of designing backgrounds, I started using press type. The work got better and I was slowly getting more calls. So, needless to say, I was spending a lot of time at home.

JK: How did it come about? How many flyers would you be doing in a week?

BE: Sometimes two or three a week, something like that.

JK: And when did it switch so you started getting paid for it? Were Baron and Breakout already paying?

BE: They were paying but they weren't paying. I was getting very little money—five dollars, fifteen dollars, you know?

JK: So a lot of the time there would be a party that would have your flyer, but you wouldn't show up at the actual gig?

BE: Sometimes, yeah. And then after a while there was a time, like in '79 for a couple of months, I wasn't going to any jams. I just stayed home, made the flyers. And then they were always talking about, "Oh, you gotta go, you gotta go." Because, like I said, I wasn't really that type. I just made the flyers, stayed home. And then finally I went to one—this was maybe around March of '79—and I noticed that it was different because they sounded different. They sounded a bit more polished. Of course, I'm referring to the Funky Four. And after that I decided, okay, maybe I'd better go again, you know?

JK: So when the first records came out, and when "Rapper's Delight" got on the radio and all that—how did people in the inside community like yourself feel about that?

BE: That's a good question. Me, I didn't really have too much of a feeling about it because I'd heard one or two things on the radio. Because mostly at the time, everything was just on tape, so we'd hear sometimes people on the bus with tapes, when people go by carrying the box with the tapes. The first thing I can remember hearing on tape was "King Tim Personality Jock." And then I heard Sugarhill. But when I heard Sugarhill, I'd heard Big Bank Hank's rhyme and I was, like, yeah, he's biting off of Caz. Because in fact, I heard Caz do that rhyme at the PAL back in '79. And then after that I heard the Sugarhill record.

JK: Tell me more about when we're starting to move toward '81, '82, '83, that sort of thing. Did the community aspect of this start to drag more, or what happened? Did the shows get bigger? What was it like a little later, like in '81 and '82.

BE: In '81 and '82—that was when they had the so-called "Downtown scene," which I wasn't a part of. So a lot of times what I did was just make flyers for Armstrong, and he gave a lot of parties out of state.

JK: What, like Connecticut, Jersey, that sort of thing?

BE: Yeah.

JK: But you didn't hit the downtown scene?

BE: No, that wasn't me. You'd be better off talking to Phase about that.

JK: And then, go even later than that—we're starting to talk '82, '83. That's when it seems like a lot of the originators were kind of fading from the scene.

BE: Yeah, you can say that.

JK: Why do you think that was?

BE: Why? I think certain people were maybe looking for something different. That's what I think it is.

JK: And this was just like a phase of your lives that had passed?

BE: Yeah, you had that and then you had other people coming up. That was around the time 1982, 1983, that Run D.M.C. starting coming out, and then the Sucka MCs—that must have been about 1983. And then after that began the decline of the old school.

JK: I agree with that, because I think once Run D.M.C. came around it was a different art form. When did you make your last flyers?

BE: My last one was—let me see—I was doing one for Rodney C back in '84.

JK: But that was pretty much it.

BE: After that, yeah. People stopped calling. I mean, it wasn't like I was trying to do anything else after that. It was just that I sort of faded from the picture, you could say.

JK: How do you feel about the renewed interest in your artwork now, people like me showing up?

BE: I find that to be very strange, because it's twenty years and change, and to be honest with you, I never thought anybody would be interested.

A PICTURE
IS WORTH A
THOUSAND
MOVES

Jorge "POPMASTER FABEL" Pabon

"Yes yes y'all and ya don't stop! Rock on 'til da break of dawn!" This common vernacular blasted through enormous homemade speakers and echoed across neighborhoods, alerting all to the devastating sounds of our cultural imperative. Furious rhythms bounced and ricocheted off tenements and project buildings, penetrating the souls of the youth and calling them to arms. Young, restless, and bursting with the spirit of self-expression, they looked out their windows, fire escapes, and front stoops in an effort to locate the epicenter of this explosive sonic boom. Charged with adrenaline, these urban soldiers prepared themselves for artistic warfare. In battle mode, they adorned themselves with urban armor. The tools of their trade included: fly kicks, starched and pressed denim jeans, matching shirts with ironed-on letters or painted graffiti designs, and their heads topped off with colorful crowns. Customized gear identified their crews and tribes.

Bound by a common purpose, they made their ways to the sacred grounds: the powwows, the jams. On this call to duty, b-boys and b-girls rounded up their troops by whistling and calling out codified chants. Once again the streets witnessed an unquenchable passion inherited from ancestors who celebrated life and death similarly. Putting their bodies on the line, risking injury and humiliation, New York City youth rose from the ashes of burned down tenements and transformed into a mighty Phoenix flying through clouds of ecstasy toward a burning sun of self-empowerment. We developed self-discipline and self-motivation against all odds in the true school of hard knocks.

Growing up in New York City during the 1970s and 1980s left an immense impression on me that can hardly be expressed in words. If I were capable of transferring my experiences and visions onto a screen, the world would be utterly amazed. Certainly many others saw and experienced the same and even more. Street life was always full of surprises. Every turn and twist of this concrete labyrinth challenged us and kept us ready to rock steady. Extreme intensity molded our personalities and characters. Even casual conversations were often expressed by hand gestures and body language. Finger snaps, hand claps, and foot stomping became physical punctuation. Intricate hand shakes and embraces spoke louder than words. Facial expressions revealed temperament and approachability.

Itching for a scratch, we were dying to get into something and catch a groove. We anticipated block parties and community events. Although most events happened organically and unannounced, prearranged jams were advertised by way of homemade flyers or word-of-mouth. Narrow hallways and tenement lobbies became our dance studios and rehearsal spaces. Small parks and 'jungle gyms' were our boot-camp training grounds—swinging on monkey bars, pumping swings high and flipping off of them, stick ball, kick the can, ringolivio, double dutch, hop scotch, hot peas and butter and Johnny on the pony. We constantly found ways to entertain ourselves and to escape the troubled world around us. As a popular break song puts it, "Children playing, women producing, men go to work and some go stealing. Everybody's got to make a living." We tried to make heaven out of hell.

My earliest memories of rockin' and b-boyin' are of young outlaws challenging each other in the streets. On my block, in the early 1970s, we had a gang that up-rocked called the Savage Samurais. In 1976 we had a b-boy crew called the Floor Master Tops, younger brothers of the Savage Samurais. These rebels possessed a fierce attitude and swagger. B-boys and b-girls were very charismatic and projected a strong sense of pride and confidence. 'Ghettoriginality' permeated their essence as they proudly positioned themselves on street corners and front stoops. Dancing to the drummer's beat, they got on the good foot executing steps, moves, and combinations with impeccable timing and the utmost finesse.

There was no half-stepping back in the day. If you came, you had to come correct. The code of the culture warranted street smarts and strategic thinking. We had to earn our stripes the hard way by gradually gaining respect and credibility. B-boy/b-girl hierarchy determined who could rock in a cipher versus who had to stay on the sidelines. Acknowledging the potential repercussions, we played our positions and didn't violate circle etiquette. Within the chaos there was order.

Dancer's pulses increased with the intensity of the break beats. Heartbeats harmoniously rode the rhythms erupting into flurries of movement. We all knew when and where the breaks of the songs were. Anticipating these musical crescendos turned us into dancing timebombs. Instantly bodies would all simultaneously drop. From top-rocks to floor-rocks the breaks assaulted our senses. We had to give it up or turn it loose in order to stay on top of our game. With rockets in our pockets we flipped and tumbled, adding an arsenal of aerial assaults to our repertoires. The freshest b-boys/b-girls knew how to add just enough gymnastic flavor to the recipe without compromising

Popmaster Fabel, photo © Henry Chalfant

the integrity of the dance form. Too much "fairy flying" would lead to humiliation and major disrespect. There is a science to the dance. B-boys/b-girls became rhythm technicians. A magnificent force put us in a trance with DJs as the spin-doctors. We were furious rockers groovin' to get down.

I was raised on East 123rd Street in Spanish Harlem. Just a ten-minute walk across the Third Avenue Bridge left me about as south of the Bronx as you can get. We were a family of five: Mama Dukes (Nilda), older sisters Aida and Noemi, and my twin brother Pete. In 1977, at the age of twelve, Pete and I started venturing into the Bronx. We rode our Apollo five-speeds, chased by packs of junkyard dogs, and we explored yet another devastated urban wasteland. We realized that the South Bronx shared the same flavor and street life as El Barrio.

That same year Noemi dated Arnaldo "Tito" Cepeda, also known as Fly T, who was a DJ for The Wicked Wizzards. The Wizzards also included Kool Pat, Raymond R the Superstar, and legendary aerosol artist Phase 2. Pete and I finally got to witness hip hop architects constructing beats and rhymes up front and personally.

One hot summer day, Fly T took us to a Wicked Wizzards jam in the plaza at Betances, a housing development in the Bronx. In our eyes the Wicked Wizzards were the epitome of true school hip hop. They jacked electricity from the lamppost, set up shop and rocked the spot. Microphones were plugged into echo chambers and the speakers were stacked high. Raymond R the Superstar gripped the microphone and checked the volume. "One two, one two two two…"

The b-boys/b-girls grew restless as the verbal delay of the echo chamber added to our excitement. Already exposed to b-boy/b-girl culture in Spanish Harlem, we were able to easily identify them at this jam. Their auras gleamed

and their posturing was classic. Blaring speakers projected lyrics from the disco song, "Hot shot, hot shot, hot"—then, with a vengeance, the percussive break sent the dancers into a frenzy!

Baseball caps were turned backwards or at an angle. Flipped up hems on bell-bottom Lee Rider denims showcased blitz speed footwork. Multicolored layers of tube socks created psychedelic streaks and patterns as a result of the blurry, scrambling leg motions. It was a frantic situation! Huge afros and push-backs seemed to bounce a beat behind those who proudly wore them. It was the equivalent of taking a small super-ball and throwing it at full force into a broom closet. The movement was unpredictable and extremely dynamic. The jam had just begun and immediately there was electricity in the air. Everybody was going off!

The Bronx gave birth to a multitude of b-boys/b-girls and dance crews. The B-Boys, The Twins, Salsoul, Starchild La Rock, The Bronx Boys, Crazy Commandos, The Disco Kings, Seven Deadly Sins, Rock Steady Crew, Sasa, El Dorado Mike-Mike, D. ST., Beaver, Swane, Weebles, Lil' Boy Keith, I Spy, and Rubberband. It was very common to practice more than one element of the culture. Many legendary DJs and MCs started off as dancers. Pebblee Poo, Grandmixer DXT, Grandmaster Melle Mel, Grandmaster Caz, Almighty KG, DJ Jazzy Jay, Grandwizzard Theodore, King Pin Shahim, and Pow Wow. Most of the founding fathers of the Universal Zulu Nation, hip hop's earliest and longest-lasting grassroots organization, were b-boys known as the Zulu Kings. Eventually the planet got rocked as these renegades of funk went looking for the perfect beat.

One of my best friends at the time, Winston, moved from El Barrio to the Michelangelo housing complex on 149th Street, just off of the Grand Concourse. Pete and I made new friends in this neighborhood—Dennis, Doreen, George, Jared, Eric and Joe. Some of these friends were urban daredevils who fearlessly jumped from one roof to another, hitched rides on the back of trains and buses, jumped off second-story rooftops and from one platform to the other on the 149th Street train station. Others built go-carts, customized bicycles and roller skates, and became local skateboard kings.

Among them Joe Conzo, also known as Joey Kane, was always armed with a 35-mm camera. He rocked a monster afro and was very softly spoken. Most of us were not concerned with archiving and capturing the moment. We were too busy living it to think about saying, "Hey, bring a camera along so we can take flicks of our experiences." Thank God one of us did. Joe's instincts and passion for photography gave us the opportunity to look back and ponder the glory days. Because of his artistry we have physical proof of stories that would otherwise be too fantastic to believe. Little did we know the impact his visions would have in the future.

Viewing his work transports me into the true golden era of Hip Hop. I can taste the vibrations, hear the static, and feel the power of the most significant renaissance in contemporary American art. His photographs are timeless and invoke a spirit of celebration and truth. Joe took the time to truly appreciate the magical world of hip hop and was considerate enough to share it with the world. I'll never forget attending jams where the legendary Cold Crush Brothers would always shout him out on the microphone, "We got Joey Kane in the house!" The beauty of it all is that with the release of this publication, you can say that too.

"Joey my brother, rock on 'til the break of dawn!"

Bound by honor and loyalty,
Jorge "Popmaster Fabel" Pabon
Vice President of the Rock Steady Crew
Member of the Supreme World Council of the Universal Zulu Nation
Honorary Member of the Electric Boogaloos

WHAT YOU WRITE?

Carlos Mare 139 Rodriguez

What you write? A strange question to ask anyone when it would be more appropriate to ask, "What is your name?" But in the world of writing, or graffiti as it is commonly known, it is the first question that gets posed. If someone asks me, "What you write?" and I say, "Mare 139," they would know my tag and the street where I live. My tag represents my skill level and associations with other writers and crews and it is also a generation marker, whether I am old-school or new.

Taki 183 is widely regarded as the most influential pioneer of hitting up in the early 1970s in New York. Taki 183, being from 183rd Street in Washington Heights, was influenced by other early writers such as Julio 204, Frank 207, and chiefly Cornbread and Cool Earl from Philadelphia, who brought over the concept of getting your name up in the late 1960s. The idea that a name or mark could say so much directly and indirectly about you, and could be put up indiscriminately, seen on any street or train, was revolutionary for New York City—but not in the annals of human history.

The caves of Lascaux in France bear 17,000-year-old paintings which illustrate humanity's earliest behavior and living conditions. Ancient Pompeian graffiti included word usage and caricatures, as did public art of early Greek, Egyptian, Mayan and other civilizations of the past. These periods are vital to our understanding of where we are with modern graffiti. It is safe to say that future generations will one day excavate and find a Stay High 149 tag or an IZ The Wiz piece that will reveal something of times past. In the cases of Cornbread and Taki 183, their names remain the legacy of a whole sub-culture, past, present, and future.

Assuming a *nom de plume*, a b-boy name, an MC alias or DJ title, was a by-product of an emerging sub-culture collectively called hip hop. The idea of creating a self-styled identity with a discipline was unique to anything the world had seen before. For graffiti, the emphasis on the name was the principle identity, then the importance of style-writing became paramount. If you had a great name and great style, your standing in the community would be exalted—this was the case with Stay High 149, who was prolific and unique with his infamous tag and stick-figure character, which he borrowed from the 1970s TV show *The Saint*.

The 1970s produced many unique writers with names such as Super Kool 223, Super Strut, Box Top 149, Cliff 159, and many others. Most writers in the era were foundation writers—the writing was crude and unrefined. Super Kool 223 is considered to have created the first masterpiece, in which he broke from the bounds of a stylized tag to a more developed framework, where a fill-in color and design could decorate his name.

This period of experimentation gave birth to the foundation of style writing. Among the most notable of the pioneering era are Riff 170 and Phase2 (now known as TRUE 222). They innovated upon what would ultimately be called "wild style," the complete abstraction of the letter form by use of lettering styles with arrows and design, as opposed to plain signature styles. Phase2 created "softies" (bubble letters), which were the catalyst for the modern throw up, a quick-action fill-in and outline piece. Writers like Pistol

and Flint 707 contributed with the addition of 3-Ds to their masterpieces—this was groundbreaking, as the idea of depth and mass would influence many of the best style-writers and even my work as a sculptor.

The advancement of style writing was driven by competition and influences from neighboring boroughs. Since some subways ran from one borough to the next, the effect was immediate, and fueled creative alliances and rivalries. One of the most infamous alliances would be The Fabulous Five, which included LEE, Slave, Slug, Mono, and Fred. They would produce many whole-car end-to-end productions, notably the Christmas cars, where they painted ten whole trains top to bottom for the Christmas holiday. As for rivalries, one of the most contentious was between The Magnificent Team (TMT) and Crazy Inside Artist (CIA), two style-writing crews which sought to dominate the 2 and 5 train lines with the best wild-style productions and name coverage inside the cars. This battle took to crossing names out, and escalated to the physical over bragging rights, but masterpieces painted on the outsides of train cars were respected.

With the rise of competition in the 1980s came the battle for space and respect. Writers held their tags and masterpieces as sacred monikers, so if you tagged over someone the consequences were that all your tags and pieces would be crossed out—or you'd get beaten up. In this era, the environment for writing became more hostile from within the writing community. The transit authorities and government officials that wished to erase every single name on the transit system were gaining the upper hand. At the same time, the popularity and distribution of name writing became more of a phenomenon, not just locally but nationally and globally, along with the other disciplines of hip hop—b-boying, DJ-ing, MC-ing. The viral effect was unintentional and unstoppable, as it ushered in a new generation of writers and enthusiasts to the hip-hop culture.

An art form that started as an informal communiqué amongst children of the ghettos became the voice and visual dialogue of a disenfranchised youth movement worldwide. Interests from galleries and from media and law officials became influential to the development of the art form. Since it started to become more inopportune to create whole cars and wild-style masterpieces against the train buffs and the cross-outs, some writers retired and others sought out opportunities in the fine-arts and commercial worlds, thus re-branding their names and identities.

This ushered in what I call "commercial bombing," the idea of getting your work or your tag associated with corporate identities to gain a broader audience for yourself as well as financial endorsement. Initially, writers like Crash, Zephyr, Revolt, Haze, Cey, and Futura 2000 led the way in this effort—in his work with the rock group The Clash, for example, Futura 2000's groundbreaking creative style broke with the tradition of what graffiti art was and should be. His whole train work *Breakout* redefined subway painting, aerosol painting, and design for years to come: it was absent from traditional wild-style writing and focused on his painting and design techniques. A new signature was born.

Carlos Mare 139 Rodriguez (photograph © Henry Chalfant)

Through the late '80s, subway graffiti continued in the absence of the great style masters. In many ways, though the art form hit a void for some years in the development of its style, it nonetheless expanded in terms of ideas and networks beyond New York City. As the buff conquered the subways and the names faded into memory, something new took the place of the mass transit system, a far greater and further-reaching system to get up on—the internet.

My brother Kel 1st and I were the first to adapt to this technology in 1989. We realized its potential and the parallels to getting up or getting art and information to the global masses with minimal effort. Initially it was modest and crude, no "dot coms," no multimedia, but the freedom of publishing and creativity was undeniable. It was the force of the future to come, to an extent that no one anticipated, but we predicted its affect on our generation. We saw that if we could share our history through photos and copy we could have a broader influence on the documenting of our culture and our art form. What was once a Mare 139 tag became mare139.com, and this revelation became more and more important to preserving my legacy.

The world has dramatically changed with technology: it supercedes our wildest dreams within the writing culture, it transcends boundaries faster than ever, and it offers artists a creative passport to other artists and countries, much like the subway system did for writers in New York City. Today's network is robust and diverse through the net, but more importantly we see more and more images and photos of early formative subway graffiti. We have a database of our past to reference, and this, my friend, is the beauty of it all—that it allows for the preservation of names and styles that shaped not just me but a whole global movement.

Writing—hitting up, getting up, graffiti, vandalism—holds a continual effect on the world at large and its personal and artistic purpose is always evolving. It is many things to many people, yet it is more of its past than its future. I am not any different than I was then, in many ways—I still want to get my name up, I still want to be associated with Kel, Crash, Dondi, Duro, K56, Noc 167, Min One and others, and I still have my heart in the struggle of 139th Street in the South Bronx. So maybe, if you ask me what I write, the answer may be that I write my history: I write Stay High 149, Super Kool 223, LEE, Phase2, Riff 170, Chain 3, Part 1, and Mare 139.

Carlos Mare 139 Rodriguez

THE LAND BEFORE THE RHYME

Disco Wiz

Disco Wiz

I am the prodigal son
And I was born on holy ground
Yes it's true I come from Mecca
But I am the product of many
And I am no one and no one in me
Then again I am all that can ever be
You see the streets sang to me
Sweet urban lullabies
I am the product of kings and
    queens
Mayan Aztec Taino dreams
That never die
I am that spicy version of your
    American apple pie

I am a product of uprisings
    revolutionary
Movements and my ancestor's cries
If you choose to swim in these
    waters
Be ready to die! 'Cause you might
    have to
Some things in this life are just
    worth that much

Walk with me
As I decipher these scriptures
Struggles of my time
The land before the rhyme

Structured in the mind
No need for the nine
This complex life of mine
1975, the movement has arrived

Funny, of this no one can speak
a subject all too deep
A childhood that seems lost,
never had the means to floss,
abandoned by this cause

Often despised
even criticized
How would I surmise
To this my only prize

No ends could be made
For the price we would pay
Economically strapped
No time for a nap

'Cause this is about to go down

The boogie down was burning
And my people yearning
Just to get a piece of the pie
My mind's eye
Was as big as the sky

So who's to blame
For the circumstances aimed
At the unspoken names?
Pawns to the game
This shit remains the same

The city with no fate
A place to escape
183rd, oh you never heard?
Now that was the place to be

To see poetic street warriors
Turntable masters
Childhood dreams of mine
An art form divine
A land before the rhyme

We wired our systems to a
    lamppost
DJ battles for years to boast
The stage was set
Here comes the test
The chosen ones to be so blessed
Two turntables above my chest
A mixer cued to do the rest
This would be the weapon of
    choice
This music speaks, it is our voice

The beauty of it all to be
This life we leave for you to see
For things that were just what they
    seemed
We knew of who we were to be
But lived for more than what we
    dreamed

For what you sow, you reap
A junkie for a beat
In the parks I creep
The perfect scratch I seek
We ruled these fucking streets

A pioneer, you say
From way back in the day
No royalties to pay
No riches came our way

No faking the funk
As the base would thump
The treble got me high
My revolution has arrived

Hip hop supreme
No cheddar, no bling
Guided by knowledge
No need for the cream

So tell me now
Can you answer this riddle?
Never have so few
Done so much for so little

We spit you out to chance
In a b-boy stance
Never to realize
What would be the prize

Who would have known?
Industry now owned
Globally world-known
Our baby is full-grown

And although the legend goes
We birthed this flow
But who the fuck are we?
Nobody knows

Call me the mixer
For the mixer is me
I rock the speakers
And the speaker is me
You seek the teacher
The teacher is me
I am hip hop
And hip hop is me

Luis Cedeño a.k.a. DJ Disco Wiz
Hip Hop's First Latino DJ